Royal Navy Aces of World War 2

SERIES EDITOR: TONY HOLMES

OSPREY AIRCRAFT OF THE ACES® • 75

Royal Navy Aces of World War 2

Andrew Thomas

OSPREY
PUBLISHING

Front cover
In the final weeks of 1944, the Royal Navy despatched the powerful British Pacific Fleet for service against the Japanese alongside the US Navy. Formed around its heavily armoured aircraft carriers, and initially based in Ceylon, the British Pacific Fleet was requested to conduct a series of strikes against the vital Japanese oil facilities in Sumatra during its long voyage to its operational base in Australia. The first target to be hit was at Pangkalan Brandan, in northern Sumatra, which was attacked on 4 January 1945 as part of Operation *Lentil*. One of the three carriers on this strike was HMS *Victorious*, part of whose fighter element comprised 1834 and 1836 Naval Air Squadrons (NASs). Both units were equipped with Corsair IIs.

Among the pilots in 1836 NAS was 20-year-old Canadian Sub Lt Don Sheppard, who was a veteran of the strikes against the German battleship *Tirpitz* in Norway the previous year. The main strike for *Lentil* launched from the ships some one-and-a-half hours after the fighter sweeps, and Sheppard, at the controls of Corsair II JT410, formed part of the close escort to the Avenger bombers of 849 NAS. The escort remained with the bombers to the target, which, as expected, was heavily defended by the Japanese.

Both flak and fighters met the strike force, and at 0850 hrs over the sea near Pangkalan, Sheppard spotted a Ki-43 'Oscar' just below him. He immediately closed on the enemy fighter, which initially dived away in a vain attempt to escape, before pulling up and trying to out turn the Corsair II. Sheppard described the subsequent events in his combat report;

'The Jap's cockpit seemed to glow as I hit him with a long burst, and I could see the bullets hitting the engine and cockpit. He levelled out at 300 ft and then went into a climbing right hand turn. I fired again and the pilot baled out as the aircraft rolled over and went into the sea. I watched the pilot land in the water, but he appeared to be dead.'

Ten minutes after claiming his first air combat victory, Sheppard spotted another 'Oscar' over the target, and once again he closed in before opening fire with the Corsair II's battery of six 0.50-cal guns. The lightly built Ki-43 blew up under the sheer weight of fire and crashed into the sea. Don Sheppard then headed back to *Victorious*, having claimed the first two of an eventual six kills, which would make him the most successful Commonwealth pilot in the Corsair. He would achieve acedom in the British Pacific Fleet's final strike on Sumatra on 29 January, and claim his sixth, and final, victory during the Okinawa campaign on 4 May (*Cover artwork by Mark Postlethwaite*)

First published in Great Britain in 2007 by Osprey Publishing
Midland House, West Way, Botley, Oxford, OX2 0PH
443 Park Avenue South, New York, NY, 10016, USA
E-mail: info@ospreypublishing.com

ISBN 978 1 84603 178 6

Edited by Tony Holmes
Page design by Tony Truscott
Cover Artwork by Mark Postlethwaite
Aircraft Profiles by Chris Davey
Index by Alan Thatcher
Originated by PDQ Digital Media Solutions
Printed and bound in China through Bookbuilders

08 09 10 11 12   12 11 10 9 8 7 6 5 4

For a catalogue of all books published by Osprey please contact:
NORTH AMERICA
Osprey Direct, C/o Random House Distribution Center,
400 Hahn Road, Westminster, MD 21157
E-mail:info@ospreydirect.com

ALL OTHER REGIONS
Osprey Direct UK, P.O. Box 140 Wellingborough, Northants, NN8 2FA, UK
E-mail: info@ospreydirect.co.uk
www.ospreypublishing.com

ACKNOWLEDGEMENTS
In addition to many friends and fellow enthusiasts, too numerous to mention, who have generously given support to bring this volume to fruition, the author wishes to record his gratitude to the following who gave of their time in answering queries and presenting accounts of their actions for inclusion within this volume: Capt E M Brown CBE DSC AFC, Sir Malcolm Guthrie Bt, B Heffer DSC, Lt Cdr P R Sheppard AFC, the late Cdr J W Sleigh DSO OBE DSC and the late Capt G C Baldwin CBE DSC & bar.

CONTENTS

A NAVAL 'FIRST'

The formation of the Royal Air Force as an independent air service on 1 April 1918 meant that the Royal Navy lost control of its air arm, the Royal Naval Air Service. It was not until 24 May 1939 that it regained full control of the Fleet Air Arm, a title that still remains in use today. Just a matter of months earlier, in October 1938, the Royal Navy's embarked fighter squadrons had begun receiving more modern equipment when 800 NAS was issued with its first monoplane, the Blackburn Skua. 803 NAS had followed suit by year-end. Then, in February 1939, 801 NAS received the Fleet Air Arm's first single-seat Sea Gladiators, with 802 NAS getting them in May. The previous month, a few examples of the Skua's turreted cousin the Roc had also entered service.

None of these types were particularly effective, but the Skua was nonetheless better armed than its predecessors, having four wing-mounted machine guns. However, the aircraft was woefully underpowered, for its Bristol Perseus XII engine gave the fighter a maximum speed of just 225 mph. The Roc was even worse, for the bulk of its turret reduced the type's maximum speed to barely 200 mph, although in practice it was less. Lt Donald Gibson, who was to achieve some success in the coming war, remembered;

'The Gladiator was a wonderful aeroplane to fly but the Skua was downright comical, being remarkably unstable in some respects. I liked it because you could actually see in front of you on the landing approach, which helped a lot if you were only an average pilot. Both aircraft were of little use in the fighter role because the enemy was better equipped. The Gladiator was manoeuvrable, but did not have enough speed to catch the enemy. The Skua was the deadly medium, being a little faster but not as manoeuvrable.'

The main fighter in use with the Fleet Air Arm at the start of World War 2 was the two-seat Blackburn Skua, which also doubled as a dive-bomber. It was Skuas of 803 NAS, to which this formation belonged, that achieved the first confirmed British aerial victory of the war, and they later achieved some notable successes over Norway in 1940 (*P H T Green Collection*)

The other fighter type embarked in Royal Navy aircraft carriers at the start of the war was the biplane Gloster Sea Gladiator, which equipped just one frontline unit. This one belonged to 769 NAS, which was the Fleet Air Arm's advanced training unit. One of the squadron's instructors at the time this photograph was taken was future ace Lt 'Bill' Bruen (*J M Bruen*)

When war was declared on 3 September 1939, the Royal Navy had seven aircraft carriers in service – HM Ships *Argus* and *Hermes*, both of which were small, the larger *Furious* and *Eagle*, the fleet carriers *Courageous* and *Glorious* and the recently delivered *Ark Royal*. Of these, only the latter two had fighters as part of their air groups. *Glorious*, based in the Mediterranean, had 802 NAS's Sea Gladiators aboard, while in the Home Fleet, *Ark Royal* had the Skuas of 800 and 803 NASs embarked. 801 NAS had disbanded during the summer to become the basis of 769 NAS for advanced fighter training.

The carriers were soon active enforcing the sea blockade of Germany and conducting anti-submarine sweeps. On 14 September two of *Ark Royal*'s Skuas from 803 NAS had attacked a U-boat but were damaged by their own bombs and forced to ditch! Later that same day, *Ark Royal* narrowly avoided being hit by torpedoes, but 72 hours later *Courageous* became the first British warship to be lost in the conflict when it was sunk off the coast of Ireland by U-29. Some 518 sailors perished.

With the Fleet Air Arm having suffered its first losses, revenge for 803 NAS was not long in coming, for on 26 September the Home Fleet sailed to cover the daring escape of the damaged submarine HMS *Spearfish* from German waters. In the late morning, some 250 miles north-west of the German island of Heligoland, three Dornier Do 18 flying-boats were sighted and Skuas were launched to intercept. The Dorniers made off, pursued by the Skuas that at first had difficulty in locating the intruders against the dark sea background. A sub-flight of Skuas from 800 NAS, led by Lt Finch-Noyes, fired off all their ammunition at one Do 18 without noticeable effect – the flying-boat continued to turn in tight circles just above the sea, before eventually escaping with one of its companions. However, the third Dornier was attacked by a trio from 803 NAS, as unit CO Lt Cdr Dennis Campbell recalled;

'A British submarine patrolling off Heligoland had been damaged in some way, and she was having trouble getting home. The Home Fleet was therefore ordered down to the Heligoland Bight to escort her back. Ahead of the fleet as it sailed south were two large cruisers, followed by the battleships *Nelson* and *Rodney*, with *Ark Royal* third in line, and escorting destroyers all the way around.

Left and below
The vanquished. Although of poor quality, these photographs were taken on 26 September 1939 from the deck of the destroyer HMS *Somali* as it closed on the Dornier Do 18 forced down by 803 NAS's Skuas (*Evening Post*)

'It was a perfectly clear day in the North Sea, and we had not been going long when we were picked up by three Dornier Do 18 flying-boats, which circled around the fleet on the horizon. Nine Skuas from 800 and 803 NASs were immediately launched in a free take-off, with each sub flight of three aircraft attacking a different shadower. We rushed to the attack with great delight, and thinking this was our big chance, we blazed away with the only ammunition we had – 0.303 ball. This was unlikely to do much damage unless we hit something vital, but one of our sub flights was successful, as one bullet went through the radiator of a Dornier, which had to come down in the water due to the loss of its coolant.'

In a notable 'first' for the Fleet Air Arm, Lt B S McEwen and his gunner Petty Officer (PO) B M Seymour, along with Lt Charles Evans and his observer Lt W A Robertson, were credited with the first enemy aircraft of the war to be confirmed destroyed by British forces. Their victim was Do 18 K6+YK of 2./KuFlGr 506, flown by Leutnant zur See Freiherr von Reitzenstein, who, with his crew (one of whom was seen waving his white overalls) was picked up by the destroyer HMS *Somali*. The aggressive Evans was described thus by a colleague;

'Known as "Crash" Evans or "the flying Christ", he was probably one of the greatest Fleet Air Arm characters of all time, with his flaming red hair, pointed beard and piercing blue eyes.'

The first British air combat success was also Charles Evans' first step to becoming an ace.

One of the pilots who shared the first victory was the fiery haired Lt Charles Evans, who went on to become an ace during 1940 (*via B Cull*)

THE EARLY ROUNDS

After the initial skirmishes, *Ark Royal* then sailed to Freetown, in what was then British West Africa, to participate in the hunt for the German pocket battleship *Graf Spee* in the South Atlantic. However, when the raider was scuttled in December, the aircraft carrier returned to Scapa Flow.

To protect the main Home Fleet anchorage, a site at Hatston, in Orkney, was developed as an airfield. At the end of November 1939, 804 NAS was formed there with Sea Gladiators under the command of Lt Cdr J C Cockburn, this unit being specifically charged with the air defence of Scapa Flow. A flight was also detached at Wick, on the mainland. On *Ark Royal*'s return, its Skuas also disembarked to Hatston.

Through the winter and spring of 1940, enemy bombers regularly made reconnaissance flights over Scapa Flow that were countered by RAF and, sometimes, Royal Navy fighters. On the evening of 20 March, future ace Lt E W T Taylour of 800 NAS was leading a section of Skuas just south of Orkney when he spotted He 111s as his combat report described;

'While acting as leader of "Green section", escorting Convoy ON 21, Kirkwall portion, I sighted about ten Heinkel He 111Ks approaching the convoy from the north-east. I immediately put my section into line astern and attacked the nearest enemy machine. I succeeded in getting a good shot, and held it long enough to fire all my ammunition. The enemy machine, as soon as I started firing, started to climb up to the cloud base where I lost him. The enemy bombing was disorganised by the Skuas, the bombing being made at random.'

However, 40 minutes later, 803 NAS's 'Blue' section was more successful east of Copinsay, as its leader, Lt W P Lucy, described in his handwritten report;

'Returning from convoy escort, my observer noticed firing to port. We investigated. A single enemy aircraft, pursued by three Hudsons, was seen some way away. We gave chase, but lost the enemy just before we were in

Skua L2933/K of 803 NAS is prepared for launch from HMS *Ark Royal* when operating in the South Atlantic in late 1939. The vessel was searching for the German pocket battleship *Admiral Graf Spee* at the time. This particular machine was usually flown by Lt Ken Spurway, who was to make five claims flying Skuas, including 2½ enemy aircraft destroyed (*G A Woods*)

range. We chased it into the clouds, and "Blue 2" parted company. Returning towards base, we observed an enemy aircraft front gunning merchant ships. I got into position above the enemy before he spotted me and delivered an attack. I overestimated the enemy's speed and closed to about 50 yards, being then thrown off my sights by the slipstream. I turned and then delivered another attack. Again I closed too rapidly, firing short bursts, and was finally smothered in oil from the enemy. The enemy was still climbing slowly with undercarriage down when he disappeared into the clouds. I fired 400 rounds from each gun. Short bursts on each attack.'

The 29-year-old Bill Lucy, who was CO of 803 NAS, was credited with a He 111 probably destroyed – the first claim for the man destined to become the Fleet Air Arm's first ace. The Heinkel was from 2./KG 26, and it crash-landed at Dulmen on its return. A second He 111 was damaged in one of the few combats involving an 803 NAS Roc.

Although the units based in Orkney only had sporadic contact with the enemy, the Fleet Air Arm's fighters were about to face a much sterner test.

DEFENDING SCANDINAVIA

On 10 April 1940 the Germans invaded Denmark and Norway, with the assault on the latter country being heavily supported by most operational elements of the Kriegsmarine. At Bergen, the force was spearheaded by the light cruiser *Konigsberg*, which then moored alongside in the harbour. Flying from Hatston at the limit of their range, 16 Skuas (five from 800 NAS and eleven of 803 NAS) led by Lt Bill Lucy carried out a dive-bombing attack. They achieved three direct hits and two near misses with their 500-lb bombs, and the cruiser sank at its moorings. *Konigsberg* thus became the first major warship sunk by air attack during war.

That evening the Luftwaffe struck back when Ju 88s and He 111s attacked shipping in Scapa Flow. Six Sea Gladiators were launched to defend the base, and the skipper of 804 NAS shot a bomber down over Orkney. A second aircraft was damaged during this action, which saw several future aces experience their first taste of action – including POs Albert Sabey and Alfred Theobald, who later became the Royal Navy's only non-commissioned aces, and Lt Donald Gibson, who recalled;

'The raid was notable for the fact that one of our pilots, in the middle of the battle, in the dark, landed and urinated on the runway, thereafter taking off again to rejoin the affray. This was probably due to a barrel of beer we had been drinking before the raid, as we had not been expecting the enemy!'

Hatston's Skuas conducted further raids to the Bergen area and sank the transport *Barenfels* on the 14th. Two days later they encountered enemy aircraft whilst escorting the damaged cruiser HMS *Suffolk*. Skuas from the recently reformed 801 NAS, as well as 803 NAS, inflicted some damage on the attackers, and a future ace opened his account when the latter unit's Sub Lt Noel Charlton (nicknamed 'Fearless Freddie' by his colleagues) claimed a share in the destruction of a He 111.

A short while later, a second section from 801 NAS downed Do 18 K6+FH of 1./KuFlGr 406, flown by Ltn zur See Keil. One of the pilots involved in this engagement was Canadian Lt W H 'Moose' Martyn, who thus claimed the first of his five kills.

French *Chasseurs d'Alpine* guard Lt G R Callingham's Skua L3048/B of 803 NAS after it had force-landed on a sand spit near Namsos on 25 April 1940. Earlier in the sortie he had shot down a He 115 seaplane. The Skua was later blown up where it stood as it could not be salvaged (*ECPA*)

At the time of the German invasion *Glorious* was in the Mediterranean, and the aircraft carrier was recalled to the Home Fleet – it arrived at Scapa on the 21st. The next day, *Ark Royal* embarked nine Skuas and two Rocs from 800 NAS and nine Skuas and three Rocs from 801 NAS. 803 NAS's 11 Skuas went aboard *Glorious*, which also embarked Sea Gladiators of 802 and 804 NASs and 18 Gladiators from the RAF's No 263 Sqn, which were to be flown ashore in Norway. The force sailed soon afterwards.

The British landings at Namsos and Aandalsnes, intended to take the major port of Trondheim, were supposed to be given air cover by No 263 Sqn's Gladiators flying from the frozen Lake Lesjaskog near Aandalsnes. These were to be backed up the Skuas, while the Sea Gladiators protected the fleet offshore. The cruiser HMS *Curlew* had been specially fitted with an air-search radar in order to support the fleet's air defences, and on the evening of the 23rd its radar detected three enemy bombers. Two sections of Skuas were launched and damaged a He 111 after conducting the first radar-controlled interception at sea.

The following day, in improving weather, *Ark Royal*'s Skuas patrolled over Aandalsnes and Trondheim, where some crews encountered the Luftwaffe. During the early evening, a patrol led by Lt Bill Lucy (in L2925) had split into two sections of three, and each had sighted a He 111 that they attacked. 9./KG 4's 5J+AT, carrying the *Gruppenkommandeur* of III./KG 4, belly-landed after being shot up, whilst a 4./KG 4 fell in flames, although one of the Skuas was also forced down. Having just claimed his first victory, minutes later Lucy, with Lt Christian, attacked and damaged another bomber that they identified as a Do 17, although it was probably He 111 5J+JT of 9./KG 4, which crash-landed at Oslo upon its return. The first carrier fighter action over Norway had been a success.

That afternoon No 263 Sqn's Gladiators flew ashore, but the lack of facilities and enemy attacks meant that most were unserviceable within 24 hours. Thus, Skuas from the carriers stationed 100 miles offshore had to maintain fighter patrols over Namsos and Aandalsnes, although they too suffered considerable losses, with the range from the ships being a significant factor.

Mid morning on 26 April, 801 NAS launched six Skuas to patrol over Aandalsnes and Lake Lesjaskog, where Lt 'Moose' Martyn damaged a He 111 that was also hit by Lt Cdr Bramwell. Feldwebel Gumbrecht's 5J+CN of 4./KG 4 crash-landed on a bleak mountainside, but it was eventually recovered and now forms an important exhibit in the Royal Norwegian Air Force Museum.

As this action was taking place, three more Skuas led by Lt Bill Lucy in L2963/F left *Glorious*, and these too encountered further Heinkels from I./KG 26 that were attacked. However, Lt Filmer's Skua was hit by return fire and force-landed with a dead gunner. Lucy and Lt Christian then attacked L1+KT of 9./LG 1 (again identified as a Do 17) and forced it down into Romsdalsfjord.

Enemy pressure, combined with the paucity of air cover, decided the fate of the Namsos expedition, and on the 27th it was decided to evacuate central Norway. Naval fighters remained active over the area throughout the day, claiming no fewer than nine German bombers destroyed and two more damaged. One raid was even driven off by the Skuas making dummy attacks as they had used up all their ammunition! HMS *Glorious'* Sea Gladiators also got their first taste of action when, at 0935 hrs, three from 804 NAS, with another from 802 NAS, caught a reconnaissance He 111 of 1(F)./122 low over the water about 20 miles from the fleet. Led by Lt R M Smeeton, their fire hit the intruder, but it gradually drew away in spite of bouncing off the wavetops three times. Badly damaged, the bomber crash-landed near Trondheim.

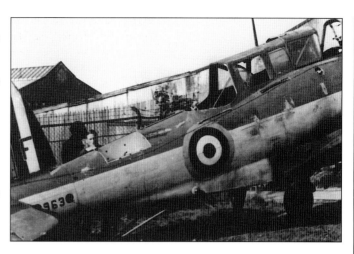

Skua L2963/F of 803 NAS was shot down during the disastrous 13 June 1940 raid on *Scharnhorst*. On 26 April it had been flown by Lt Bill Lucy when he shot down an He 111 to claim his second victory on his way to becoming the Royal Navy's first ace of World War 2
(*Birgar Larsen via Bengt Stangvik*)

Allied forces at Aandalsnes continued to come under heavy enemy air attack, and in the early afternoon, two Skuas from 803 NAS, flown by Lt Bill Lucy and PO Johnson, caught Oberleutnant Steinback's He 111 and shot it down onto a hillside near Romsdalsfjord. They then recovered onto *Ark Royal,* as *Glorious* had withdrawn to refuel.

The 803 NAS Skuas had been replaced on patrol by five more from 800 and 801 NASs, who encountered further enemy bombers. Another Heinkel was shot down over Romdalsfjord, the aircraft falling to the guns of Capt Partridge (Royal Marines), Lt Hurle-Hobbs and Lt Taylour – the latter also shared another probable, although this was apparently later upgraded. Ted Taylour, who had received a DSC for the *Konigsberg* attack, thus became the latest naval pilot to begin his path to acedom.

As this action went on, a further section from 801 NAS was launched, and just before dusk it attacked a lone He 111 from 2./KGr 100, flown by Unteroffizier Rippka. One of the Skua pilots was Lt Ronnie Hay (Royal Marines), who recalled his first combat patrol, led by Lt Bill Church;

'We ran into a He 111K bomber. Bill attacked from astern and the bomber dived to sea level. They exchanged fire, and when Bill pulled upwards to break off the attack, his aircraft was struck in the belly and crashed into the sea without survivors. I had learned my first lesson in air fighting with a vengeance – never break away upwards. I therefore sat on the tail of the bomber and fired short bursts until it crashed into the sea.'

The only member of the Royal Marines ever to become a fighter ace had just claimed his first victory, which he shared with PO Kimber.

Yet further enemy bombers were encountered over the coast, and yet another He 111 (flown by Feldwebel Werner Schulz) was claimed destroyed by an 801 NAS section which included Midshipman (Mid) George Baldwin, who was flying Skua '7H';

'We had launched to cover the first evacuation from Norway, and it was one of my first operational patrols. Over the very rugged and snow covered coast, we spotted several aircraft that the formation leader identified as 'Heinkels' and he ordered us into a line-astern to make an attack on one of them. I dived in turn, and through my inexperience probably opened fire at far too great a range, although I did at least see some hits on its seemingly enormous wings.'

FIRST ACE

Having launched from *Ark Royal* at lunchtime on 28 April to cover an evacuation convoy, Lt Bill Lucy's section soon spotted a Ju 88 bombing a ship. Lucy immediately attacked, firing a short burst. PO Johnson also made a good attack and the Junkers was reported to have crashed. Half-an-hour later, this section attacked some He 111s that approached the convoy, and in concert with Sub Lt Brokensha, Bill Lucy shot one down into the sea near Molde. This was his fifth confirmed victory, and he thus became the Fleet Air Arm's first ace of World War 2, even though the term was not recognised by the Admiralty in London.

The pair then chased still more bombers that in turn ran into a section from 800 NAS. One of these Heinkels was shot down by the three Skuas from the latter unit, Lt Ted Taylour claiming a share in the victory, as well as helping to damage another He 111 that later force-landed. Yet more bombers were then sighted, and with their remaining ammunition, the 803 NAS Skuas engaged the enemy. Lucy and Brokensha again combined to shoot down a He 111, the 8./KG 26 machine flown by Unteroffizier Liesske force-landing near Sunndalsfjord.

With *Glorious* and its Sea Gladiators withdrawn, the Rocs aboard *Ark Royal* were to provide fleet defence, and 801 NAS launched its three turret fighters twice during the day after German shadowers were spotted. Lt Ronnie Hay, with Naval Airman (NA) Bass, led Sub Lt J E H Myers and NA P Bolton and Midshipman George Baldwin and Leading Airman (LA) Smailes after one pair. However, they could only drive the bombers off. Many years later, Hay recalled the aircraft's inherent problem;

'Soon, we spotted a Ju 88 reporting the fleet's position. Diving down at maximum speed, we got to within 200 yards of the bomber – but I had no front guns, so I attempted to slew my aircraft to enable the turret to bear. Shouting "Fire!" to the gunner, I heard one bang – and silence. All the guns had jammed. The German flew off with a startled puff of brown smoke from his engines.'

George Baldwin had similar recollections of the encounter;

'Even in a dive with my throttle fully open, I had real difficulty in getting ahead or even abeam of the bombers to allow my gunner to open fire. It was so frustrating!'

The sighting report led to further Luftwaffe interest, and later in the day the Rocs were again launched, but after two hours airborne the crews returned frustrated. The carrier then left to refuel, so giving its exhausted aircrew some well-earned rest.

Ark Royal then met up with the replenished *Glorious,* still carrying its Sea Gladiators, and returned to Norway on 1 May to cover the final stage of the evacuation. They were soon located by four Do 17Ps of 1(F)./120 that were intercepted by two Sea Gladiators of 804 NAS. However, the Dorniers had raised the alarm, and a strike force was launched. Both carriers were subjected to a series of attacks by Ju 87 Stukas, during which

One of the few pilots to fly the lumbering Roc turret fighter operationally from a carrier was Lt Ronnie Hay, who later became the Royal Marines' solitary ace (*via B Cull*)

Glorious, in particular, was very lucky not to be hit. One attack was made by six Ju 87Rs of 2./StG 1 in the early evening, and in a combined patrol flown with 804 NAS, Lt Marmont of 802 NAS brought one of them down, as Lt Cdr Cockburn of the former unit later wrote;

'At 1825 hrs, six Ju 87 dive-bombers were sighted three miles ahead on an opposite course in open "V" formation. The order was given to open fire, and the section half-rolled individually onto the tails of the aircraft, each pilot attacking one enemy. Fire was maintained in short bursts, as the enemy twisted and turned, until the final bombing dive was commenced. The attack was broken off at this point, as I imagined, quite erroneously, that the pom-pom fire would take effect below this.'

The threat of air attack was now so high that there was no alternative than for the carriers to withdraw, leaving Aandalsnes and Namsos to be evacuated without air cover. However, *Ark Royal* would be back in Norwegian waters within a week.

During the evacuation of the central Norway expedition, Sea Gladiators from 804 NAS, embarked in HMS *Furious*, provided fighter cover for the fleet. One of the aircraft involved was N2276/H, which is thought to have been the aircraft flown by Lt Cdr J C Cockburn when he damaged a Ju 87 on 1 May 1940 (*R C Sturtivant Collection*)

NORWAY – THE FINAL TRAGEDY

On 4 May *Ark Royal*, with 23 Skuas of 800 and 803 NASs embarked, left Scapa to cover the Anglo-French expedition that had landed in northern Norway to secure the port of Narvik. The vessel arrived in the area on the 6th and its Skuas began patrols, encountering the Luftwaffe for the first time the following afternoon. Leading Lt Russell into battle, 803 NAS's CO, Lt Bill Lucy, later reported;

'Sighted two He 111s slightly below on parallel course. Carried out an attack, after which one Heinkel dived steeply away – two Skuas from 801 NAS were then seen to join the attack. Carried out attack on remaining enemy – two Skuas of 801 NAS also attacked this aircraft, which finally escaped due to superior speed. At 1555 hrs, returning towards home, I sighted two He 111s. After one short attack ammunition was expended.'

Although Russell had been hit and had to ditch early on in the action, a Heinkel was claimed by 801 NAS crews.

Now alerted to *Ark Royal*'s presence, the Luftwaffe set about finding the vessel the following day. Despite being hunted, the carrier continued to send patrols out over Narvik and Ofotfjord on 8 May. Late that afternoon, a trio of Skuas – one of which (L2916/H) was flown by Sub Lt P N Charlton – from 803 NAS attacked a large Do 26 flying-boat, which force-landed and was destroyed by its crew. Noel Charlton's second success was, however, marred when his aircraft suffered an oil pump failure and he was obliged to ditch in Ofotfjord.

Deteriorating weather then halted virtually all flying for several days, during which time few enemy aircraft were seen. Meanwhile, HMS *Glorious* and HMS *Furious* sailed for Norway from Orkney with RAF Gladiators and Hurricanes embarked, although the former also retained the Sea Gladiators of 802 NAS for self-defence, whilst *Furious* relied on the six biplane fighters of 804 NAS.

During the early hours of 14 May, *Ark Royal*'s Skuas covered a landing near Narvik and were then active throughout the day. Attacking a group of He 111s, Bill Lucy, in his regular aircraft L2925/F, damaged one and shared in the destruction of another from Stab II./KG 26. However, the only pilot to claim more than five victories in the Skua was then caught in crossfire from other He 111s and his aircraft exploded and fell into the sea. Lucy, the Royal Navy's first ace of the war, and his observer, Lt Michael Hanson, were both killed. Donald Gibson, who later became an admiral, described his CO as both 'heroic and a brilliant fighter pilot'.

More bad weather precluded much flying on the 15th, but on the 16th it improved enough for the German bombers to reappear, thus keeping the naval fighters busy. With Narvik outside the range of German single-engined fighters, the Luftwaffe employed twin-engined Messerschmitt Bf 110 and Ju 88 *Zerstorer* in the area. One formation of six Ju 88 fighters was engaged over Rombaksfjord by 803 NAS just as the enemy sighted the Royal Navy force. The sighting of the ships led to a further big dogfight in the afternoon, during which two Ju 88s and a He 111 were brought down – a considerable achievement for the Skua crews.

Further skirmishes followed, and by the time *Ark Royal* withdrew to refuel on the 17th, its Skuas had claimed three Ju 88s, a He 111, a Do 17 and a Do 26 destroyed since arriving off Narvik. Nine Skuas and one crew – that of the unfortunate Lucy – had been lost, however. The other two carriers arrived offshore at this time, and on the 21st they began disembarking the RAF fighters to Bardufoss, whilst the Sea Gladiators also patrolled the area. *Ark Royal* returned to Scapa on 26 May, and two days later three of 802 NAS's Sea Gladiators, flown by Lts Feeny, Lyver and Ogilvie, shot down a He 115 which broke up on hitting the water. Narvik fell to the Allies the next day.

Despite this success, the stunning German advances in France and the Low Countries following the launching of the *Blitzkrieg* on 10 May meant that Allied priorities had changed, and the exploitation of gains in northern Norway was now impracticable. As a result, *Ark Royal* and *Glorious* returned to cover the Allied evacuation of Narvik on 2 June, with troops commencing their pull out the following day. More inclement weather initially protected the withdrawing forces, but as it improved, the Skuas flew ground attack missions to cover the evacuation.

During the early hours of the 8th, surviving RAF Hurricanes and Gladiators from Nos 46 and 263 Sqns flew aboard *Glorious*, which then set sail for Britain. However, that afternoon the carrier and its escorts were intercepted by the battlecruisers *Scharnhorst* and *Gneisenau* and all were sunk with great loss of life, including the whole of 802 NAS. However, the *Scharnhorst* was hit by a torpedo fired by HMS *Acasta* – an event that was to have a profound effect on the naval fighter force.

Whilst *Glorious* was being sunk, *Ark Royal* was busy escorting a convoy from Narvik. During the evening of the 9th a formation of bombers was intercepted and the He 111 flown by Oberleutnant Bocking of 5./KG 26 was shot down by a section led by Lt Donald Gibson, who made his first claim, as did PO Alf Theobald.

When news reached the Royal Navy that the damaged battlecruiser *Scharnhorst* had berthed in Trondheim for emergency repairs, a strike by 15 Skuas (six from 800 NAS and nine from 803 NAS) was hastily

The Royal Navy's first 'rating' ace was PO Alf Theobald, who made his initial claims in early June 1940 whilst flying Skuas with 803 NAS off Norway (*J W Sleigh*)

launched from *Ark Royal* on the night of 12/13 June. Split into two formations, the Skuas had to fight for their lives through flak and defending Bf 109 and Bf 110 fighters. Eight were shot down, including the aircraft flown by both COs, and the survivors only escaped by desperate low flying in the early morning mist. One of the survivors was flown by Lt Donald Gibson, who recalled in his memoirs;

'We approached Trondheim harbour in a shallow dive. Pat Gordon-Smith, my observer, in his matter of fact voice told me that four Messerschmitt 109s were astern of our section, and I could see four Messerschmitt 110s on my starboard side. I could also see Skuas going down as I led my section down. This bombing attack could be compared to the Charge of the Light Brigade.'

He evaded and was the last of the survivors to land on the carrier.

Gibson commented later that 'Ideally, all future admirals should be shot at in an aeroplane while they are still young!'

DUNKIRK

On 1 February 1940, 806 NAS was formed under Lt Cdr Charles Evans with Skuas and a few Rocs for service aboard the new carrier HMS *Illustrious*. Soon afterwards, however, Evans had most of his experienced pilots posted and replaced by men fresh out of training. His senior observer, Lt Desmond Vincent-Jones, remembered their arrival;

'The look on the CO's face was unforgettable and horrific, but first impressions can often be deceptive. Little did we imagine what distinction this strange group would achieve in the months ahead. Ivan Lowe was the senior member, and the other sub lieutenants were Stan Orr and Frank Buttle, and the midshipmen included Jackie Sewell, Graham Hogg and John Day. At least two of them hadn't started shaving, but within a year most of them would have DSCs pinned to their chests.'

Together with Evans and his remaining flight commander, Lt Bill Barnes, four of the newcomers would soon become aces.

During the Norwegian campaign 806 NAS flew a few attacks on Bergen from Hatston, before returning south to Worthy Down, but early on 28 May the unit as alerted for an immediate move to Detling, in Kent, to help cover the evacuation of the British Expeditionary Force from the beaches at Dunkirk. It was a traumatic day, as Desmond Vincent-Jones recalled;

Skua L3011 joined 806 NAS when it first formed, and was part of the detachment sent by the unit to help cover the evacuation of the Dunkirk beaches. The fighter flew its first sortie off the French coast on the evening of 28 May, with squadron CO Lt Cdr Charles Evans at the controls (*P H T Green Collection*)

'Our first section, under Lt Campbell-Horsefall, took off from Detling consisting of two Skuas and one Roc. The latter, crewed by Mid A G Day and NA Jones, crashed on take-off, although neither was hurt. Within 20 minutes we were told that this section had been shot down and we were to replace it immediately. Graham Hogg managed to limp into Manston with his aircraft riddled with bullets and his air gunner killed.

He travelled back by train in his flying clothing, and was arrested by a zealous military policeman for being an enemy parachutist!

'Feeling as if we were living through some frightful nightmare, and still suffering from intense hangovers, the CO and myself took off, accompanied by a further Skua and a Roc. Deciding after what had gone before that discretion was the better part of valour, we accepted the advice to patrol further from the shore, and to take advantage of available cloud cover – and so survived.'

It seems that the first section, flying an unfamiliar type wearing naval grey camouflage, had been attacked by 'friendly' fighters. During the following afternoon, a patrol comprising a pair of Skuas and a Roc, led by Lt Bill Barnes, spotted five Ju 88s attacking a convoy off Ostend. They attacked, claiming one bomber shot down and sending another limping off and losing height with serious damage. Lt Vincent-Jones was on hand again to describe what is thought to be the Roc's only confirmed victory;

'The only significant achievement of 806 NAS was when a section surprised Ju 88s lurking over the line of ships. The Skuas attacked from above, attracting the attention of the German aircrew, while the Roc, piloted by Mid Day, flew directly under the Junkers and, as described by Skua pilot Lt Barnes, "Literally sawed it in half with the four guns in its turret firing upwards". We all then landed safely at Detling.'

806 NAS was joined on 31 May by a detachment from 801 NAS, which mainly flew dive-bombing sorties, and they immediately suffered losses to marauding Bf 109s that same day. One of its surviving pilots was Lt Ronnie Hay, who recalled being 'on one operation over the Channel

It is thought that the lumbering Roc achieved only one confirmed victory – a Ju 88 (misidentified at the time as an He 111) downed near Dunkirk by an 806 NAS aircraft on 28 May 1940. Prior to seeing combat off the French coast, L3105 had been flown by several notable pilots whilst they were working up with the squadron (*P H T Green Collection*)

Also active over France was 801 NAS, to which L3003 belonged. Note that the underside of its port wing has been painted black as an identification feature. This particular machine was almost certainly flown by Lt Ronnie Hay on 31 May, when his formation was attacked by Bf 109s (*P H T Green Collection*)

coast, where it was thought from a distance that a Spitfire escort was about to join us. The "Spitfires", however, had black crosses and only four of us from 801 NAS got back. I was chased by a Bf 109 until finally shaking him off over North Foreland'.

The fight, however, was not completely one-sided, as NA L W Miles, the gunner flying with Lt W H Martyn, shot down the Bf 109 flown by Unteroffizier Werner Francke, who was killed. Two days later, nine aircraft from 806 NAS, led by Lt Cdr Evans (in L2989/L6A), had another encounter during a morning patrol. Evans reported;

'Observed a stick of four bombs dropped ahead of a British cruiser, thought to be HMS *Coventry*. It is thought that the enemy escaped in low cloud. At 1052 hrs a Ju 88 was observed and was attacked by A Flight of 806 NAS, and the enemy was seen to pass through tracer. The bomber went into a spiral to the right and disappeared through the cloud towards the water and was possibly destroyed.'

Skuas from both units continued flying over France for a time, with 801 NAS's detachment returning home on 27 June after further losses.

BATTLE OF BRITAIN ACES

To help alleviate a critical shortage of pilots in the RAF, in the middle of 1940 the Fleet Air Arm was asked for volunteers to be seconded to Fighter Command, and the first arrived in frontline squadrons on the eve of the Battle of Britain. Amongst their number was Sub Lt Francis Dawson-Paul, who was posted to Spitfire I-equipped No 64 Sqn at Kenley. On 1 July he became the first of the seconded pilots to claim a kill when he participated in the destruction of a Do 17. He wrote at the time;

'As "Blue 2", I was ordered to scramble with "Blue Section" at 1830 hrs to patrol base at 20,000 ft. I first reported a streak of white smoke, which I identified was condensing exhaust gases coming from what I thought was the enemy aircraft. This streak was about 14 miles ahead, and to the starboard of me – I was about two miles behind "Blue 1", as my engine was not giving full power.

'Crossing the coast, I passed one section of Hurricanes, and as I drew nearer I saw another section in line astern preparing to attack. "Blue 1" was also preparing himself for an attack. I concluded that the enemy aircraft must have sighted the Hurricanes and "Blue 1", as it started to take evasive action and lost height in a steep spiral. I followed down, drawing towards it, and after the Hurricanes and "Blue 1" had delivered their attack, I overhauled it and opened fire at approximately 150 yards, closing up to about 50 yards as I gave it three bursts. I saw my bullets enter the rear portion of the enemy aircraft. I broke away to port, gained height and delivered another attack from the rear.

'This time the enemy aircraft turned to port and I broke to starboard, and I was just positioning myself for another attack when I saw the enemy aircraft strike the water and sink almost at once. My aircraft was hit four times, twice in the starboard mainplane, and twice underneath the rudder. I returned to Kenley at approximately 1955 hrs.'

That same day Royal Navy pilots Sub Lts Dickie Cork and 'Jimmie' Gardner and Mid R J Patterson joined Hurricane-equipped No 242 Sqn, commanded by the legendary Sqn Ldr Douglas Bader. Also flying Hurricanes, but with No 213 Sqn, was Sub Lt Denis Jeram, who made his

The first Royal Navy pilot to become an ace whilst on secondment to the RAF in the summer of 1940 was Sub Lt Francis Dawson-Paul, who briefly flew Spitfires with No 64 Sqn from Kenley. Having claimed 7$\frac{1}{2}$ kills between 1 and 25 July 1940, he was shot down over the Channel on the latter date by a Bf 109E and fished out of the water by the crew of a German E-boat. Dawson-Paul had suffered grievous wounds during the engagement, and he died on 30 July 1940 (*CCB*)

first handling sortie with the unit the next day. Jeram flew his first patrol in what became his regular mount ('AK-U') on the 9th when he participated in two patrols off Bolt Head in response to the Luftwaffe concentrating its attacks on coastal convoys in the Channel.

At No 242 Sqn, the naval pilots quickly made a good impression on Bader, and it was 'Jimmie' Gardner who, on 10 July, claimed the unit's first bomber when some 25 miles off Lowestoft. He later described the events that unfolded;

'We went into the cloud at 2000 ft, and at about 20,000 ft we were still flying wingtip to wingtip and it was getting very bumpy. In the end I felt I just had to break away, which I did, otherwise I might have run into the other aircraft. I then circled my way down to the ground, looking for a gap in the cloud. To be frank I had never attempted blind flying in my life, but that's the way it was in war – you just got on with it.

'I came out over a small convoy of freighters going up the east coast and there was a He 111 bombing them, its greenish grey camouflage showing up against the sea and clouds. I was able to latch onto him as he quickly dived back for the Dutch coast, having spotted me. I must admit I had to go full throttle and then break the emergency boost to get more power and catch him up. I fired when within range, and he went down halfway between the English and Dutch coasts. I suddenly found my windscreen covered in oil, and thought that with all that extra power I had damaged my engine. I was pretty perturbed, so I headed back home very quickly. But I realised, as I turned west, that it was oil from the Heinkel I had been shooting and not mine.'

Two of the Royal Navy pilots who joined No 242 Sqn became aces – Sub Lts Dickie Cork (left) and Jimmie Gardner (right). Both men would later increase their scores in the Mediterranean (*Tim Graves*)

No 242 Sqn Hurricane I V7203/LE-T was regularly flown by Sub Lt Jimmie Gardner from mid July, although he made no claims with it. RAF ace Plt Off John Latta (a Canadian) was shot down and killed whilst flying V7203 over France on 12 January 1941 (via *G R Pitchfork*)

An unidentified pilot from No 64 Sqn runs for his Spitfire I at Kenley in July 1940 (*No 64 Sqn Records*)

Later that day Sub Lt Dawson-Paul became involved in an action with Bf 110s over Dover and destroyed two of them to make him the first of the seconded Royal Navy pilots to become an ace with the RAF. His was, however, a brief glory, for on the 25th, having destroyed a Bf 109 and taken his total to $7^1/2$ kills, he was in turn shot down. Although picked up by an E-boat, Dawson-Paul died of his wounds five days later.

The day after Dawson-Paul had 'made ace', Denis Jeram of No 213 Sqn experienced his first combat when he downed a Ju 88;

'On patrol, we sighted large numbers of Ju 88s, so I opened fire on one, silencing his rear guns. He then dived suddenly, letting out a length of wire attached to a parachute. He continued his dive, with petrol, oil and smoke issuing forth. I broke away and opened fire on another. His starboard engine caught fire and he dived towards Chesil Beach. I fired several short bursts at another enemy aircraft, and returned when out of ammunition. The second aircraft was definitely destroyed.'

Having been credited with a destroyed and a probable, the following day, when south of the Needles at the controls of P3585/AK-Q, Jeram shot down a Bf 110. By mid September he had four kills to his credit, but he had to wait for more than two years to gain his all-important fifth!

Another of the naval pilots to fly Spitfires was Sub Lt Arthur Blake, who served with No 19 Sqn, where he was naturally nicknamed 'Admiral'. One of his contemporaries said of him, 'Arthur was not a "gung ho" press on fighter boy beloved by the press at the time. He was quietly spoken, justifiably self-confident and amiable with all ranks in the squadron, without being patronising. He was a brave and capable pilot'.

His long time pre-war friend was Dickie Cork of No 242 Sqn, who, over Hatfield at 1700 hrs on 30 August, experienced his first combat as he described in a letter to a friend;

'The suddenness and speed of the fight took me by surprise, and it was all I could do to keep up with my flight commander. As we came down, the sky seemed full of black crosses, and whichever way we turned Nazi bombers seemed to block our way, but we hit them hard and sent them skidding in all directions. Their fighter escorts were pretty useless, and seemed more concerned with protecting themselves. In the ensuing fight we managed to destroy 12, but most of the action and my own contribution remains a blur.'

Sub Lt Jimmie Gardner's regular aircraft with No 242 Sqn bore a suitably nautical decoration – the signal flags for Lord Nelson's famous order during the Battle of Trafalgar! (*Tim Graves*)

His first combat was, however, successful, and he was credited with a Bf 110 destroyed and a share in a second.

Arthur Blake made his first claim on 3 September, when he damaged a Bf 110 over Colchester. Two weeks later, with the Battle of Britain at its peak, he shot down a brace of Bf 109s over Canterbury to become an ace – a status Cork had achieved 48 hours earlier on what is now celebrated as 'Battle of Britain Day' (15 September), as he described;

'We were attacked from above and behind by a number of Me 109s. The order was given on R/T to break formation, so I broke sharply away with an Me on my tail. I was now in a dive and suddenly flew through the second squadron in the wing formation and lost the enemy machine. At the same time I saw a Do 17 on my starboard, flying north-west. I dived 6000 ft to attack it and fired a long burst at the port engine, which started to smoke. I attacked again on the beam – large pieces of the enemy machine flew off and his starboard wing burst into flames near the wing tip. He dived straight into the cloud, heading towards a clear patch, so I waited until he came out into the open and fired another burst in a head-on attack and the machine dived into the ground.'

'Jimmie' Gardner was not far behind him in achieving ace status, for on the 18th, over the Thames Estuary, he was credited with the destruction of two Do 17s to take his total to five. Both he and Cork were soon

The second Royal Navy Spitfire ace was Sub Lt Arthur Blake, who flew with No 19 Sqn. He too was killed in action before the end of the Battle of Britain (*via C F Shores*)

decorated with the DSC. However, on 29 October 'Admiral' Blake failed to return from a patrol. His CO, Sqn Ldr Brian 'Sandy' Lane, himself an ace, wrote 'It is a great loss to the squadron, as he was very well liked by all, as well as a pilot of exceptional ability'.

Some 58 naval pilots were seconded to serve with Fighter Command – 12 made claims and four became aces during the Battle of Britain, and another subsequently. However, seven of them were killed and two wounded – a high price.

MEDITERRANEAN BATTLES

The declaration of war by Italy against Britain and France on 10 June 1940 immediately threatened the main sea route to the Empire that ran through the Mediterranean via the Suez Canal. Also threatened was the strategically vital island of Malta. In the Mediterranean, fighters of the Fleet Air Arm fought some of their fiercest engagements, and each of the fleet carriers deployed was severely damaged by enemy action, with two, plus an escort carrier, sunk.

When war with Italy began, the only aircraft carrier in the Mediterranean was HMS *Eagle*, which had no fighters embarked. However, its Commander (Air), Cdr Charles Keighly-Peach (nicknamed 'K-P'), promptly took steps to rectify this situation, and on 18 June the ship's Fighter Flight, parented by 813 NAS, was formed with four Sea Gladiators brought out of storage from Malta.

Ironically, the Fleet Air Arm's first combat missions in-theatre were flown against erstwhile ally France, for the fate of its powerful fleet based in Algeria was of the utmost concern following the French surrender to the Germans on 22 June. Eleven days later, France rejected an ultimatum for its vessels to join the fight against the Axis or sail to neutral territory. The Royal Navy's powerful Gibraltar-based Force 'H' then bombarded the French fleet, whilst overhead, *Ark Royal's* Skuas soon became embroiled with Vichy French fighters. Lt 'Bill' Bruen of 803 NAS damaged a Hawk 75 and a Morane MS.406 over the harbour of Mers el Kebir, before leading his section to attack a Breguet Bizerte flying-boat that was shot down to enable him to claim his first victory. The harbour was attacked again on 6 July.

Upon the completion of this distasteful action Force 'H' resumed convoy operations, and on 9 July a section from 800 NAS, led by unit CO Lt Smeeton, with Sub Lt Fell and PO Sabey, attacked a shadowing Cant Z.506B floatplane. Once the latter had landed on the water, the Skuas continued to strafe it until it was totally destroyed. The Cant was the first Italian aircraft to fall to the Fleet Air Arm. Later that same day 40 Savoia S.79 bombers appeared, and Skuas of 803 NAS, led by Lt Donald Gibson, intercepted them. Flying with PO Alf Theobald was NA de Frias, who recalled;

'Gibson led the section down in a diving turn to get at them, and for

Skua L2927 of 803 NAS flies over *Ark Royal* in the summer of 1940. It was flown by Lt Bill Bruen during the attack on the French fleet on 3 July 1940, when he made his first claims. Bruen was also flying L2927 when he achieved his next victories on 31 August (*Author's Collection*)

some reason Theo didn't get a decent burst in. We ended up flying straight and level, with the enemy leader only 40 ft off our starboard beam. I could hardly believe it was happening as I opened up with the Lewis gun on a simple no deflection shot, using the nose of the enemy as an aiming point. The aircraft went into a dive and I caught a glimpse of it going into the sea.'

'Freddy' de Frias received the DSM for his efforts in the action that continued his pilot's path to acedom.

Further east, HMS *Eagle's* handful of Sea Gladiators saw their first action on 11 July when Libyan-based S.79s made repeated attacks on the fleet. Shortly after lunch, Keighly-Peach and Lt Kenneth Keith sighted a formation of five bombers and 'K-P' attacked the aircraft to the left of the formation – a 90° *Gruppo* machine from the 194ª *Squadriglia*, flown by Sottotenente Floreani – while Keith went for one on the right. 'K-P' made three attacks, closing to within 50 yards of his target and setting the bomber alight before it spun into the sea. However, return fire hit his Sea Gladiator, with shrapnel entering K-P's thigh – it was finally recovered in 1976!

Skirmishes continued, and off Crete early on the 13th, Keighly-Peach made three attacks on a shadowing S.79 out of the sun and reported flames coming from the port wing before it spun into the sea. Three hours later, he and Keith saw three more Savoias approaching from Rhodes. Both the biplanes attacked the aircraft to the left of the formation, which fell into the sea in flames. Keith destroyed yet another S.79 later that afternoon, as *Eagle's* small band of biplane fighters continued to defend the fleet. On 29 July the flight's Lt Pat Massy made the first of his six claims when he shot down one of the seemingly ever present S.79s.

Meanwhile, in the west, *Ark Royal* helped cover the first delivery of Hurricanes to Malta, these aircraft being flown off the old carrier HMS *Argus*. During this operation, a section of Skuas led by Lt Donald Gibson shot down the S.79 carrying Genrale Cagna, commander of the *Regia Aeronautica* in Sardinia.

In mid August the Mediterranean Fleet raided the port of Bardia, in Libya, and during its withdrawal, on the 17th, the vessels were subjected to bombing attack. In order to provide additional cover for this operation, three of *Eagle's* Sea Gladiators had been flown to Sidi Barrani, in Libya, prior to the raid. Flying from here during the morning of the wthdrawal, Cdr Keighly-Peach made three attacks on a bomber and saw pieces fall off and a man bale out as the aircraft rapidly lost height as it disappeared into cloud.

Later that month, during the fleet's next operation, Keighly-Peach intercepted a shadowing Z.506B, as he later described;

'Again off Crete I came across a Cant Z.506B – I think the crew must have been asleep, as I was offered no opposition, and felt almost

The first fleet fighters in the Mediterranean were the Sea Gladiators of HMS *Eagle's* Fighter Flight, formed by Cdr Charles Keighly-Peach. He made all of his claims in N5517/6-A, which is seen here landing back aboard *Eagle's* deck in July 1940 (*R C Sturtivant Collection*)

This poor, but very rare, photo is of the leading Sea Gladiator pilot, Cdr Charles Keighly-Peach, who in five successful combats claimed 3½ aircraft destroyed and one probable. A regular officer, he was awarded a DSO for his leadership of *Eagle's* Fighter Flight, which provided much needed air defence for the fleet against the *Regia Aeronautica* (*via B Cull*)

committing murder – it was too easy. The Cant ditched off the coast of Crete and I saw the crew descending via parachutes, and they must have come down close enough to land to be able to swim ashore.'

This was his fifth claim, all of which he gained flying Sea Gladiator N5517, to make him the most successful Royal Navy pilot on type.

That same day, 31 August, far to the west off the Balearic Islands, Skuas of 803 NAS, led by Lt Bill Bruen, found a Cant Z.501 flying-boat in the civil markings of *Ala Littoria*, albeit flown by a military crew. In his report Bruen wrote;

'The section patrolling at 12,000 ft was ordered to steer 090 at 10,000 ft and search for a shadower which was soon observed low down, turning away from the fleet. The section attacked from up-sun, the first burst starting a bad petrol leak in the starboard wing tank. During our attacks the enemy aircraft appeared to attempt to alight in the sea, but bounced and crashed. No survivors were observed. Flames and smoke from the burning enemy were even seen from the fleet, 16 miles away!'

At the end of August 1940 a powerful new presence arrived in the region for service with the Mediterranean Fleet in the shape of HMS *Illustrious*. She was the lead ship of a new class of carrier fitted with an armoured flightdeck – and as events would show, they were to prove their worth! Embarked was 806 NAS, still led by Lt Cdr Charles Evans, flying the first Fairey Fulmar eight-gun fighters. These were soon in action.

During an operation off Rhodes on 2 September, three Fulmars, led by Evans, cheered the entire fleet by shooting down a Cant Z.501 flying-boat. The other pilots involved were Sub Lt Ivan Lowe, making his first claim, and Lt Cdr Kilroy. However, an attack by S.79s resulted, and just before 1500 hrs Lt Bill Barnes' section intercepted them, as described by 806 NAS's senior observer, Lt Desmond Vincent-Jones. 'Barnes, as he always did, pressed home his attack until he appeared to almost ram the enemy bomber'. The first of Barnes' eight victories was shot down in flames. Also involved was another of the unit's rising stars, Sub Lt Jackie Sewell, who claimed two others, although return fire damaged his Fulmar so badly that he had to be shepherded to Malta by Bill Barnes.

One of the 806 NAS pilots to rise to prominence in 1940 was Sub Lt Stanley Orr, who by the end of the year had become an ace (*via C F Shores*)

The first victory for the Fulmar was claimed by N1886 of 806 NAS on 2 September 1940 when Sub Lt Ivan Lowe shared in the destruction of a Cant Z.501 with two other pilots from his unit (*D J Tribe*)

Off the Dodecanese two mornings later, Lt Cdr Kilroy and Sub Lt Stanley Orr shot down a Savoia S.81, while an hour later Barnes and Sewell attacked a formation of S.79s and shot one down after closing to within 100 yards of their victim.

Orr's second victory came on the 17th in the form of a Z.501 flying-boat that he recalled had 'colourful paintwork, with the top wing like a rising sun. Having attacked, the aircraft started to pull up, the pilot obviously having been killed, before it spun to destruction into the sea'.

Sub Lt Stanley Orr's second victory was this Z.501 flying-boat, which he shot down off the Dodecanese on 2 September 1940. He described it as having a 'top wing painted like a rising sun' in his combat report (*D J Tribe*)

With the fleet continuing operations in the eastern Mediterranean, another of 806 NAS's young pilots began his successful career shortly before lunch on 29 September when Sub Lt Graham Hogg attacked a Z.501 which went spiralling down in flames. *Illustrious'* fighters found more action on 12 October whilst covering a convoy to Malta that was vigorously opposed by Sicily-based bombers. Late in the morning, formations of Savoia S.79s appeared, and Lt Cdr Evans with Sub Lts Hogg and Lowe shared in the destruction of two of them close to the carrier. Charles Evans' shared claim made him the Royal Navy's latest ace, an achievement 'Jackie' Sewell achieved on 1 November – another of no less than nine pilots from 806 NAS that would become aces whilst flying the Fulmar.

Sewell's next victory, on 8 November, was somewhat different. At the control of one of the Sea Gladiators transferred to 806 NAS from *Eagle*, and in company with Lt O J R Nichols, he caught and shot down an Augusta-based Cant Z.501 of 186ª *Squadriglia*. Soon afterwards, a formation of S.79s was detected approaching the force some 150 miles east of Malta, and Lt Cdr Evans claimed one, with a second being shared with Sub Lts Hogg and Lowe.

The fleet remained under surveillance as preparations for the torpedo-bomber attack on Taranto continued. On the 10th, Jackie Sewell and Bill Barnes combined to destroy Sottotenente Ferri's Z.501, which they chased down to sea level and then strafed. This gave Sewell his seventh success, whilst the share took Bill Barnes to acedom. The following day Ivan Lowe shared in the destruction of another Z.501 to reach ace status.

In the western Mediterranean with Force 'H', *Ark Royal* now had the Fulmars of 808 NAS embarked, but it also retained 800 NAS's Skuas within its air group too. *Ark Royal's* Fulmars got their first taste of success during operations off Sardinia in early November when, on the 8th, 808 NAS CO Lt Rupert Tillard intercepted a solitary S.79. Attacking it from astern, he sent the bomber crashing into the sea. His squadron's first victory also set him on the road to acedom.

At the end of the month a major action took place south of Sardinia when seven Skuas attacked three Italian cruisers, although they only managed near misses with their bombs. However, others, including one flown by PO Sabey, shot down an Ro.43 floatplane in flames. Meanwhile, a Fulmar patrol from 808 NAS, led by Lt Ted Taylour,

The first pilot to achieve five victories with the Fulmar was Sub Lt Jackie Sewell of 806 NAS, who also claimed two in Sea Gladiators as well (*via C F Shores*)

Ark Royal's **Fulmar unit was 808 NAS, which saw much action over the western Mediterranean throughout 1941**
(*P H T Green Collection*)

caught a Z.501 after a long chase and shot it into the sea off the Algerian coast, where it blew up on impact. 808 NAS engaged more Italian aircraft that afternoon, and amongst other claims, Tillard downed an S.79.

ENTER THE LUFTWAFFE

In early January 1941 Force 'H' escorted another Malta convoy, and on the 9th 808 NAS's Fulmars encountered Sardinian-based S 79s, of which their CO shot down two. Their demise made Rupert Tillard the first Royal Navy pilot of 1941 to 'make ace', and both he and his observer, Lt Somerville, were awarded DSCs shortly afterwards. However, the balance of power in the Mediterranean was about to change with the arrival of the Luftwaffe's *Fleigerkorps X* in Italy.

In the central Mediterranean the following day, as *Illustrious'* aircraft attacked an Italian convoy, Lt Robert Henley was on CAP and reported that 'an aircraft identified as a Messerschmitt 109 attempted to join the formation, but did not attack. When it broke away, the Fulmars proved too slow to pursue it'. A little later he came across an S.79, which he shot down in company with Lt Jackie Sewell. However, as he recalled;

'The S.79s made a low pass over the fleet, which drew us off at low altitude and high speed to the southeast, and this in turn allowed the Germans to make their attack. By the time I got back, without ammunition, all I could do was to make dummy passes at them as they started their dives on the carrier.'

Attacking the fleet just as two S.79s made their courageous torpedo runs on *Illustrious* were Ju 87s from I./StG 1 and II./StG 2. Following a long stern chase, Sub Lts Stan Orr and Graham Hogg also succeeded in shooting one of the Savoias down, although it took all their ammunition to do so. The Stukas hit the carrier with six bombs, and although Sub Lt Ivan Lowe managed to get one, he was wounded by return fire and forced to ditch, with his observer dead. Lt Bill Barnes, with Lt Vincent-Jones, had a narrow escape, leaving the deck just as the bombs struck. Vincent-Jones recalled;

'When we had reached a few hundred feet we found ourselves surrounded by Ju 87s as they were pulling out of their dives. Some were very close and I could clearly see the rear gunners firing at us. I looked down and saw poor *Illustrious* passing through huge columns of water, with smoke coming from the after end of the flight deck.

'Meanwhile, Barnes had no shortage of targets – he had, in fact, too many, and contented himself with pumping bursts into Stuka after Stuka as they came through his sights – and there was no question of not being able to see the whites of their eyes! I found it difficult to see what was going on up front, but I saw one Stuka go down with smoke pouring out of its engine. The next thing I remember was Bill Barnes telling me that we were out of ammunition.'

They were ordered to land at Hal Far, in Malta, to where their battered ship limped for emergency repairs.

806 NAS's seven remaining fighters flew protective cover over Grand Harbour, as the presence of *Illustrious* acted like a magnet to enemy bombers and Malta's long ordeal entered a new and terrible phase. The Fulmar pilots still had successes, and during further raids on the 19th, 806 NAS's Robert Henley was amongst those to see action;

'I recall a fairly massive raid of Ju 87s and Ju 88s, with all available fighters scrambled – some four Fulmars – and we just flew around uncontrolled, shooting at anything that came within range. The poor old Fulmar had problems gaining height and speed against the Ju 88s. My aircraft was hit, I think to my embarrassment, by a Ju 87, which stopped my engine some miles east-south-east of Hal Far.'

Henley ditched and was rescued, and, living to fight another day, was credited with a Ju 88 destroyed.

806 NAS also acquired the remaining Sea Gladiators from the RAF's No 261 Sqn at this time, and when flying one of them on 24 January, Jackie Sewell saw tracer fire coming past his wings, followed by a Ju 88 diving towards Hal Far. Sewell followed as Lt Vincent-Jones, who witnessed the action, said, 'From the ground it gave the impression of a terrier yapping at the heels of a mastiff!'

Another who flew from Malta was Stanley Orr, who at dusk on 5 February scrambled as bombs rained down. His observer was Lt Vincent-Jones, who described getting airborne as the bombs came down;

'Orr sighted a Dornier (actually a Ju 88) silhouetted against the sunset to the west and gave chase. We made our approach from his port quarter, and another Fulmar came up opposite us and concentrated on his starboard engine. What looked like a stream of pink golf balls passed between the two Fulmars without doing any damage. It was not long before the Dornier went down into a shallow dive, with a fire breaking out in the cabin. Moments later it hit the water, which soon put the fire out. Orr was so intent on his gunnery that he only just remembered to pull out on time. At least there was no doubt about this one.'

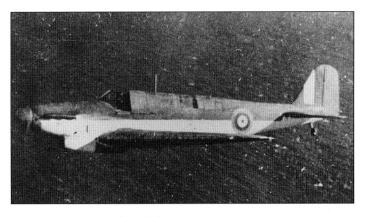

Lt Bill Barnes' observer snapped this photograph of an 806 NAS Fulmar flying on his wing during a patrol from *Illustrious* in late 1940 (*D J Tribe*)

However, Malta's skies were becoming increasingly dangerous with 7./JG 26's Bf 109Es now marauding over the island, and on 2 March three Fulmars, led by Lt Barnes, scrambled against them and all landed safely, albeit damaged. Tragically that night Bill Barnes, described as 'undoubtedly one of the finest officers and most courageous aviators that the Royal Navy has ever produced', was shot dead in error by a sentry.

CRETE

During February, 800 NAS's Skuas made their last claims, and the newest armoured carrier, HMS *Formidable,* arrived in the Mediterranean. That same month, in Egypt, 805 NAS formed with Fulmars and Buffalos. The unit was ordered to provide protection for the island of Crete, so in mid February it detached three Fulmars to Maleme under the command of Lt 'Skeets' Harris of the Royal Marines. They were soon in action.

805 NAS also embarked three Skuas, along with three from 806 NAS, in HMS *Eagle* to escort a convoy, which was attacked on the 21st by He 111s of 4./KG 26 from Rhodes. One was downed by Lt Cdr Alan Black, CO of 805 NAS, and another one fell to 806 NAS's Lt Bob MacDonald-Hall and his wingman.

Formidable had the Fulmars of 803 NAS, led by the highly experienced Lt 'Bill' Bruen, embarked, as well as some additional aircraft from 806 NAS. Its arrival in-theatre was timely, for in early March the move of almost 60,000 troops into Greece began. Crete thus became a strategically vital location in support of the Greek campaign, and its importance warranted the despatch of six more Fulmars and three Buffalos from 805 NAS as reinforcements for Lt Harris' flight.

On the morning of 19 February, three Fulmars and a Buffalo (the latter flown by Lt Rupert Brabner, who was then the Member of Parliament for Hythe) scrambled against an incoming raid. Lt Robert Kay, with Leading Airman (LA) Stockman as his telegraphist/air gunner

Lt Bill Barnes of 806 NAS, who was an outstanding officer and pilot, was tragically killed when he was shot in error by a sentry on Malta (*D J Tribe*)

During a scramble from Crete on 19 March 1941, Buffalo I AS419 of 805 NAS, flown by Lt Rupert Brabner, suffered an engine failure and overturned when landing at Maleme (*D H Coates*)

(TAG), attacked the S.79s, shooting one down and damaging two more. However, their fighter then collided with a fourth and crashed into the sea. The troopships' presence naturally attracted enemy attention, and whilst escorting a convoy on 21 March, *Formidable*-based Lt Bruen encountered a Ju 88 and sent it crashing into the sea.

On 28 March, as the Mediterranean Fleet engaged an Italian force off Cape Matapan, Lt Donald Gibson and PO Alf Theobald, again from *Formidable*, sighted a pair of Ju 88s. Theobald's observer was LA Freddy de Frias, who many years later described the events;

'The enemy fleet was just about in sight when Theobald spotted a Ju 88 below us. The two Fulmars went into a diving attack (our only chance of getting a Ju 88) and shot it down. At our speed of just over 200 knots you only got one pass. Fortunately, an Albacore observer reported seeing the Junkers going into the sea, and so a confirmed claim was allowed.'

This share made Alf Theobald the first Royal Navy rating pilot to become an ace. Below, the Battle of Matapan continued, eventually leaving the Italians routed, their battleship damaged and three cruisers and two destroyers sunk. In spite of this success, the German invasion of the Balkans on 6 April transformed the situation in Greece, and within two weeks an evacuation was ordered.

In an effort to hinder enemy operations in Libya, the Royal Navy despatched vessels to bombard the port of Tripoli. After refuelling at Suda Bay, Crete, on 20 April, the fleet sailed for Tripoli soon after dawn. That morning, a pair of 806 NAS Fulmars, flown by Charles Evans and Sub Lt Jackie Sewell, found a transiting Cant Z.1007bis, which they shot down in short order – this was Evans' tenth, and last, victory.

Two hours later a formation of five Ju 52/3m transports from I./KGzbV 9 were spotted en route to Africa, and these were attacked by two sections from 806 NAS. The first section of Lt Shears and Sub Lt Sparke was quickly joined by the other, led by Lt Henley. Four of the transports were credited as shot down – one to Henley for his third victory, one to Shears and two to Julian Sparke, thus beginning his meteoric rise to acedom, although Shears' Fulmar was shot down.

Sparke was a pre-war regular who had won a DSC flying Albacores during the Dunkirk evacuation, and he had subsequently been 'recruited' by Evans for his aggressive spirit.

As the fleet withdrew from Tripoli the following day, heavy air attacks were anticipated. A shadower was duly shot down in the early afternoon when Sub Lts Stan Orr and Graham Hogg found a Do 24N flying-boat of *Seenotstaffel 6* flying low over the sea. They quickly forced the Dornier down with its port engine on fire, and each time it attempted to take off again it was attacked and left sinking. The expected attack eventually came late in the afternoon of the 22nd, and the bombers were intercepted by 803 NAS CO Lt Bill Bruen. He led a section from his unit, with a second one from 806 NAS comprising Henley and Sparke – the latter pair shot down Unteroffizier Gerhard Pfiel's Ju 88.

With the evacuation of Greece in full flow, shipping heading for Suda Bay came under further air attacks, although Fulmars from *Formidable* and 805 NAS provided escort whenever possible.

In spite of the situation in Greece, the survival of Malta remained of the utmost importance, and at the beginning of May a heavily escorted convoy, code named 'Tiger', sailed and eventually came under attack near Sardinia on the 8th. *Ark Royal* had recently embarked a second Fulmar unit in the form of 807 NAS, and as the first raid developed, eight were launched to supplement four from 808 NAS, led by Lt Rupert Tillard.

As the fighters approached the force of 16 S.79s, they were in turn bounced by escorting Fiat CR.42s, and Tillard, attempting to dogfight with the nimble biplanes, was shot down and killed, along with his observer, Lt Somerville. Lt Ted Taylour's aircraft was also hit and his TAG badly wounded. As the bombers pressed on to the carrier, the first Fulmars from 807 NAS arrived. Lt 'Buster' Hallett waded in, hitting one of the Savoias, but his fighter was in turn struck by return fire and he was then forced to ditch. Battle of Britain ace Lt Jimmie Gardner also attacked the same S.79 as Hallett, which duly disintegrated under the weight of his final burst, thus opening the squadron's account.

Two hours later another section from 808 NAS, led by Lt Ronnie Hay (who had claimed his fifth victory the previous month), shot down an S.79 off Galita Island. As was so typical of the Malta convoy battles, the day's action was not yet over, for just before dusk another raid approached, and once again the Fulmars were scrambled. The intruders were 28 Ju 87s of I./StG 1, escorted by six Bf 110s from 9./ZG 26. The airborne section of 807 NAS went for the escort, whilst the remaining Fulmars from both squadrons attacked the dive-bombers. Lt Taylour of 808 NAS downed one of the Stukas before being hit, forcing him to limp back to *Ark Royal* with his starboard undercarriage dangling.

The other section had also enjoyed success, with Jimmie Gardner destroying two Ju 87s. However, his fighter was also badly hit, and he too crashed on *Ark Royal's* deck upon his return to the ship.

Further east, the Mediterranean Fleet was pushing westward to support 'Tiger', and it too saw some heavy fighting. Among those who claimed victories was Lt Bob MacDonald-Hall of 806 NAS, who recalled;

'We came across two He 111s, the first of which I rather stupidly flew in formation with some 50 yards behind! I still managed to blow up the Heinkel's starboard engine, however, the debris of which – being glycol and fuel – smothered my cockpit and I watched it cartwheel down and hit the sea. I then rejoined Touchbourne, and we harassed, attacked and shot down the other Heinkel, prior to returning to *Formidable*.'

A third He 111 fell to pilots from 803 NAS, led by Lt Bill Bruen. The destruction of Oberleutnant Max Voigt's 1H+FN of 5./KG 26 made him the Navy's latest ace.

Later that day, Lt Robert Henley of 806 NAS shared in the destruction of a reconnaissance Ju 88 off Cap Pessero with Sub Lt Julian Sparke, whilst MacDonald-Hall and Touchbourne found a second Junkers bomber, which they attacked and saw crash into the sea.

Bad weather then intervened, helping to shield the fleet through much of the 9th. However, that afternoon a Ju 88 from 1(F)./121 was shot down by Henley and Sparke, so elevating both pilots to acedom. Action for the naval fighters then decreased somewhat, although two days later nine Ju 88s appeared overhead. The irrepressible Julian Sparke, who in just over three weeks had become an ace, and been awarded two bars to his DSC, attacked Ju 88 L1+IR of 7./LG 1 flown by Oberfeldwebel Engel. He pressed his attack home to such a degree that both aircraft

Another pilot who attained prominence during the spring of 1941 was Sub Lt Julian Sparke of 806 NAS. He claimed six victories in less than three weeks of combat prior to being killed in action on 11 May (*C Lamb*)

collided and fell to their destruction. Thus ended Sparke's short but action-packed career as a fighter pilot.

The intense action had left *Formidable* with just four serviceable Fulmars, and with no immediate replacements, it was thus initially poorly placed to play a significant role in the forthcoming battle for Crete. The fleet returned to port on 12 May, where the dynamic Charles Evans was rested, his operational career as a fighter pilot now over.

Crete was now being subjected to increasing air attacks, and with some of its aircraft having already withdrawn to Egypt, 805 NAS was down to just two Fulmars and four Sea Gladiators. Its pilots also flew Hurricanes with the RAF's No 33 Sqn, and at dawn on 16 May some were scrambled and Australian Lt Alex Ramsay ran into Bf 109s of 8./JG 77 near Maleme, shooting down two of them. However, Maleme itself was badly bombed, destroying 805 NAS's last aircraft.

The first German paratroops began landing on Crete on the 20th, and 805 NAS's ground party participated in the defence of Maleme. However, in spite of great gallantry, an evacuation was soon ordered, and the Mediterranean Fleet – including *Formidable*, carrying a dozen Fulmars from 803 and 806 NASs – sailed for the island.

The vessels would not be seriously threatened until just before midday on 26 May, and 806 NAS's new CO, Lt Cdr Garnett, with Jackie Sewell as wingman, intercepted two He 111s. After the experienced Sewell had sent 1H+CN of II./KG 26 into the sea, the CO spotted a pair of Ju 88s. Garnett attacked first, followed by Sewell, who hit the bomber hard and caused L1+CV, flown by Unteroffizier Geisenhoff, to ditch. It was the youthful Sewell's 13th, and final victory. Return fire had hit Garnett's Fulmar during the attack, forcing him to also ditch.

As this drama unfolded, Lt Bob MacDonald-Hall and Sub Lt Graham Hogg also intercepted a pair of Ju 88s. Attacking together, they set one on fire and followed it down until it hit the sea – its destruction made MacDonald-Hall an ace. They were also credited with a second one destroyed, but this may have been the same Ju 88 attacked by the CO and Sewell. *Formidable's* fighters reported 20 combats that morning, claiming four aircraft destroyed and one damaged.

However, by a stroke of ill luck, the carrier was spotted in the early afternoon some 150 miles to the south east of Crete by a formation of Ju 87s from North Africa – II./StG 2. In the devastating attack which ensued, the Stukas scored two direct hits on *Formidable's* flightdeck,

Fulmar N1957 of 806 NAS, with Lt Bob Macdonald-Hall at the controls, helped shoot down two Ju 88s on 26 May 1941. Macdonald-Hall, who had taken off from HMS *Formidable*, duly became an ace following these successes (*via G R Pitchfork*)

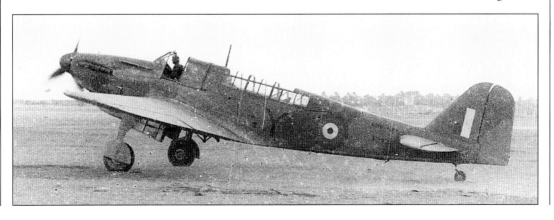

while near misses caused serious underwater damage. A pair of Fulmars damaged two of the Ju 87s, and in spite of the damage they managed to land on afterwards, but the ship had been hard hit, as had the destroyer HMS *Nubian*. By early evening the vessel was able to launch fighters once more, and it arrived safely in the Egyptian port of Alexandria.

With the carrier out of action (it would take many months to repair), air cover for the vessels evacuating Crete had to be left to land-based fighters flying from North Africa. Many miles from the Greek island, the latter were hard pressed to protect the Royal Navy, which would pay a high price in warships sunk to Luftwaffe attacks as a result.

Disembarked to Aboukir, on 28 May 806 NAS was ordered to scramble its duty flight to the Crete area. The two Fulmars (which were flown as single-seaters in an effort to save weight, and thus increase their range) were led by Lt MacDonald-Hall, and they were the first friendly aircraft seen by the ships for 24 hours.

The Royal Navy continued to endure air attacks as it continued its evacuation, and in the early hours of 1 June MacDonald-Hall and Sub Lt Hogg, covering evacuation ships inbound to Alexandria, found a lone bomber. Bob MacDonald-Hall recalled;

'We came across a Ju 88 which appeared to be a reconnaissance machine, and on that occasion we had a considerable height advantage. Although it turned towards Crete, we both attacked the Junkers and watched it spiral down and hit the water.'

The aircraft's demise was the final confirmed victory for both men, and it also made Graham Hogg the Royal Navy's leading Fulmar ace.

With a total of 12 victories, 806 NAS's Sub Lt Graham Hogg was the leading Fulmar ace. He was subsequently killed in a flying accident on 18 March 1942, aged just 20 (*via C F Shores*)

DESERT INTERLUDE

The Allied invasion of Vichy-French held Syria began on 8 June, with the Royal Navy committing a cruiser force off the coast and some of the air cover being provided by *Formidable's* fighter squadrons. 803 NAS's Fulmars moved to Lydda, in Palestine, but off Sidon during the first afternoon three were lost to nimble French fighters. In spite of these losses, 803 NAS patrolled over the cruiser force on the 10th until relieved by 806 NAS, which had been re-equipped with Hurricanes at Aboukir and then moved up to assume this task in more suitable fighters. The unit returned to Egypt on the eve of the French surrender in July.

In Egypt, the land-based Royal Navy Fighter Squadron (RNFS) was formed as an amalgam of 803, 805 and 806 NASs within No 269 Wing for the defence of the rear areas, as well as convoy escort. Its HQ was established at Sidi Haneish, with 803 and 806 NASs flying Hurricanes and 805 NAS being re-equipped with Martlets from a now defunct Greek contract. Soon afterwards the veteran Bruen was replaced as CO of 803 NAS by Lt Donald Gibson, who said of his predecessor;

'He was probably one of the best naval fighter leaders of the war. He had high standards, which he insisted upon in us, and all of us who served with him were better men thereafter.'

805 NAS of the RNFS used ex-Greek contract Martlet IIIs like AX733, which was the usual aircraft of Royal New Zealand Navy Volunteer Reserve pilot Sub Lt Don Nairn. However, it was being flown by Sub Lt W M Walsh when it shot down a Fiat G.50 on 28 September 1941 (*D Nairn*)

During the second half of 1941, 806 NAS flew Hurricanes in the desert with the RNFS. The unit's first claim was made by Lt Henry Allingham, seen here in the aircraft (Z4245) in which he achieved the victory on 21 August. He went on to claim two further kills with this fighter (*H P Allingham*)

The RNFS saw no action until 21 August, when Lt Henry Allingham engaged a Bf 110 and claimed it as a probable, although his combat report bears a handwritten note of 'Since confirmed'. The Martlets were also active, but as the only radial-engined Allied fighters in the theatre, they were often reported as Fiat G.50s, and engaged! The RNFS had its first success at the end of September whilst escorting South African Air Force Marylands to Bardia, Martlet pilots spotting three G.50s turning in on the stragglers and Sub Lt W M Walsh duly hit one, which broke up in a steep dive.

The unit had its greatest success on 20 November during Operation *Crusader,* when a flight of 806 NAS Hurricanes were top cover for a sweep. They encountered an enemy formation near Bir el Gobi, as Sub Lt Noel Charlton recounted afterwards;

'I observed the Ju 87s turning below and I dived down toward them, violently weaving on the way. I made a diving quarter attack on the port rear bomber, and after two short bursts it commenced a vertical dive into the ground, where its bombs exploded on impact. The remainder of the bomber formation increased their dive and jettisoned their bombs, and as they levelled out, I attacked the starboard rear bomber from the beam quarter. After about five two-second bursts this bomber dropped behind in a dive towards the ground, with smoke pouring from it. After seeing it hit the ground and burst into flames, I attacked the rear bomber from astern, but with no apparent results. On breaking away from this attack, I felt a slight jolt as a small burst from the rear gunner struck my aircraft, with no apparent ill effects.'

Charlton was credited with three Ju 87s shot down and another probable before being forced down by a Tomahawk. Added to his two shared victories from the Norwegian campaign, he thus became the Royal Navy's latest ace, and was awarded a DFC by the RAF for this action.

The siege of Tobruk was lifted a week later, although bitter air fighting continued over the area. On 1 December the RNFS engaged Ju 88s, and their escort, claiming four destroyed and three probables. The land-based Royal Navy pilots continued to provide convoy cover and had occasional combats over subsequent weeks, but in early 1942 its squadrons moved to the Indian Ocean to operate independently once more.

THE MALTA CONVOYS

Despite the setbacks in Greece and North Africa, maintaining Malta as an effective base remained the highest priority, and led to some of the hardest fighting of the war for the Fleet Air Arm. As well as food, fuel and ammunition, the Royal Navy also had to ferry the fighters vital to the island's defence. Thus, in mid-May 1941 after 'Tiger', a further convoy with more fighters for Malta assembled in Gibraltar and included the carriers *Ark Royal, Eagle* and *Furious.* The convoy's Hurricanes were shepherded from the launch point by Fulmars of 800X Flight, which then remained on Malta for night intruding over Sicily.

One of the pilots from 808 NAS to reach ace status in 1941 was Sub Lt Giles Guthrie, who was decorated with the DSC. He later served as a test pilot (*Portsmouth Gazette via P H T Green*)

Over Catania on 6 July, Sub Lt Mike Tritton (later a wing leader in the Far East) spotted a Fiat BR.20M with its lights on, and with a three-second burst sent it down in flames at the mouth of the Simento River. PO Albert Sabey shot another down over Catania that same night, and ten days later Tritton destroyed another bomber over Malta.

In mid July a further convoy left Gibraltar, with its escort including *Ark Royal* and its 21 Fulmars. The vessels were located by the Italians early on the 23rd and air attacks soon began. The first wave of S.79s was intercepted by 808 NAS's 'Red' section, which included Lt Giles Guthrie, who shared the destruction of a bomber with Lt Duncan Lewin. 807 NAS's CO, Lt Cdr Sholto-Douglas, led in 'Buster' Hallett, and they shared another. However, accurate return fire forced three of the Fulmars to ditch, although the crews were picked up. Later that afternoon another attack was mounted, and Lt Ronnie Hay's section downed Tenente Dolfuss' S.79. Afterwards, among others, Guthrie received a DSC.

800X Flight's Fulmars also remained active, and on the night of 1 September PO Sabey caught a BR.20 near Mount Etna. Firing a lengthy burst, he saw it go down in flames north-east of Gerbini airfield. Sabey then headed back to Malta, having become the Royal Navy's latest ace – he later received a DSM for his work. Also awarded this decoration was one of the Flight's observers, Sgt G R I Parker (an RAF NCO on loan). He later trained as a pilot and gained nine victories flying Mosquitos.

Convoy 'Halberd' sailed for Malta at the end of September, and on the afternoon of the 27th it came under attack and the battleship HMS *Nelson* was hit by a torpedo. Half-an-hour later, some SIAI S.84 torpedo-bombers arrived and Lt Ted Taylour's section from 808 NAS brought one of them down near *Ark Royal*. Others chased their prey into the gun barrage, with Giles Guthrie and his wingman bringing down another S.84 which they erroneously identified as a 'BR.20'. Later in the day Lt Jimmie Gardner's section shot down a shadowing Cant Z.506B for his tenth, and final, success. The day had seen the Italians suffer heavy losses.

As normal, the heavy escort turned for Gibraltar before reaching the 'Sicilian narrows', and shortly before midday on the 28th two sections from 808 NAS, led by Lt Taylour and Lt Hay, shot down a shadower. The unfortunate Cant was Ted Taylour's seventh, and final, success, and Ronnie Hay's last in the Fulmar.

Almost three weeks later Force 'H' sailed on Operation *Callboy* towards Malta, and during 17 October a Sardinian-based Z.506B was attacked by a section led by Lt Giles Guthrie. They shot out the floatplane's port engine and then concentrated their fire on the starboard one, after which it crashed into the sea. Guthrie had claimed his all-important fifth victory. In 1936 he had co-piloted the Percival Vega-Gull which had won the Portsmouth-Johannesburg air race, and post-war he succeeded to his father's baronetcy and also became the chairman of BOAC.

The loss of *Ark Royal* to a U-boat attack in November was a massive blow to the Mediterranean Fleet, but convoy and ferry operations continued through the winter months nonetheless, with varying degrees of opposition. However, by the early summer of 1942, as the situation in Malta deteriorated, further reinforcement became critical. A convoy – code named 'Harpoon' – was planned, with *Eagle* and *Argus* providing the air cover. The former carried 16 Sea Hurricanes of 813 NAS's Fighter

Flight and 801 NAS, as well as four of 807 NAS's Fulmars, two of which were also aboard *Argus*. A second convoy – 'Vigorous' – would sail from Alexandria, and the passage of both would be strongly opposed. 'Harpoon' entered the Mediterranean on 12 June and was located the following evening. At 1930 hrs Lt King-Joyce and Sub Lt Crosley from 813 NAS launched after a shadowing Cant Z.1007bis, as the latter duly recalled;

'I could now see the dark exhaust smoke from his three engines passing over the top of my hood as I closed in. With cloud cover only a short distance ahead, I pulled back on the stick, got his underside flying into the centre of the ringsight and pressed the firing button. As I did so, I could see sparks coming from the Cant's tail, then I could see smoke coming from the port side. I continued firing through the smoke.

'I overshot him as I turned away into the clear and could see that his port wing and engine had flames coming from them, as well as smoke. He was already turning slowly to port and losing height. When it touched the sea it left a trail of yellow pieces of fuselage behind in its wake.'

This was the first of Crosley's $4^1/2$ victories. The enemy relocated the eastbound convoy the following morning, and the same pair were airborne early. Crosley again described as he closed on Unteroffizier Schwarz' Ju 88D F6+EH of 1(F)./122;

'I pressed the firing button. The shape was wandering into my sight, huge and black, first one side then the other. I finished the entire 12 seconds of ammunition, and must have been closer than 100 yards at the end. I saw the de Wilde ammunition hitting his port wing, sparking like firecrackers. Bits of aircraft flew past me. I saw a burst of smoke from his port wing root again as the Ju 88 flew on in a shallow dive. He slowed right down – I was sure he was a goner.'

Initially claimed as a probable, the Ju 88 was upgraded to a kill when its crew was rescued and they confirmed that their bomber had indeed been shot down by Hurricanes.

Towards midday, the main Italian attack comprising around 40 S.79s, S.84s and Z.1007s, escorted by almost 50 fighters, arrived and many combats ensued. The torpedo-bombers came in first, and although some bombers fell, several ships were hit. The Sea Hurricanes then waded into the fight, with the CO of 801 NAS, Lt Cdr Rupert Brabner, engaging Macchis and Savoias at about 11,000 ft. He reported;

'Attacked a C.200 from astern, which spun down and was considered destroyed. Head-on attack on S.79 and hit seen – another attack on different S.79 and explosion in rear of aircraft and caught fire. Attacked third S.79 and hits seen on starboard wing root – bomber last seen losing height.'

Brabner was credited with an S.79 and a Macchi C.200 destroyed as the attack was broken up with heavy losses. Sub Lt Peter Twiss, later famous as a test pilot, became involved with the escort, as he later recalled;

'This was the first time I had been in combat with the CR.42, and was under the impression that they would outmanoeuvre the heavy Fulmar. With flaps partly lowered, I was able to turn inside the second aircraft and give it a long burst. The pilot turned over his aircraft and baled out.'

New Zealander Sub Lt 'Red' Duthie of 801 NAS also claimed his first victory, although he also had a near miss;

Lt Rupert Brabner of 805 NAS made his first claim on 4 May 1941 during the battle for Crete. He was the MP for Hythe at the time, and duly became an ace during 1942. Brabner was subsequently killed in a flying accident in March 1945 (*via B Cull*)

'I had just pushed the stick forwards to break away downwards when one of the crew jumped from the S.79. He missed my Hurricane by what seemed inches, and I distinctly remember that he was wearing a black flying suit with silver buttons.'

As evening approached there was further action for the tired naval pilots when nine Sicily-based Ju 88s approached. Among those launched was Brabner, who attacked one head on which was finished off by Sub Lt Peter Hutton to ensure his first victory, and his CO's fourth. Hutton then attacked two more bombers, one of which broke up and spun into the sea. There was still no let-up, however, for Sicily-based Ju 87s of the *Regia Aeronautica*, along with more S.79 torpedo-bombers with fighter escort, appeared soon after 2000 hrs, and several pilots made more claims before the cloak of darkness then gave them some relief.

The assault resumed with surface and air attacks at first light on the 15th, before the ships finally came under land-based air cover. At this point the main escort group withdrew during the night, with the action for the exhausted fighter pilots and ships' companies almost over. A greater trial was to await them later in the summer when Malta's torment reached its peak.

THEIR FINEST HOUR

With conditions on Malta becoming increasingly desperate, Operation *Pedestal* was planned. The Allies hoped to fight a convoy of 13 fast modern freighters and a tanker through the gauntlet of enemy attacks to the beleaguered island. Additional Spitfires were also to be flown off to the island too as part of this operation. A large escort was assembled which, with the intensity of anticipated opposition, included no less than four aircraft carriers, although *Furious* was to exclusively ferry the Spitfires.

Ploughing its way through a Mediterranean swell with draft screens up and Sea Hurricanes parked, HMS *Indomitable* played a key role in many of the actions of 1942 (*P H T Green Collection*)

HMS *Eagle* carried the Sea Hurricanes of 801 NAS and 813 NAS's Fighter Flight, whilst aboard *Victorious* were the Fulmars of 809 and 884 NASs and the six Sea Hurricanes of 885 NAS, under the command of Lt Cdr 'Buster' Hallett – all three units were relatively inexperienced.

In contrast, *Indomitable's* units contained a wealth of experience. Sea Hurricanes equipped Lt Cdr Bill Bruen's 800 NAS, whilst 880 NAS was led by the fiery 'Butch' Judd and had Battle of Britain ace Lt Dickie Cork as its senior pilot. Completing the carrier's fighter force was Lt Robert 'Sloppy' Johnston's 806 NAS, equipped with recently acquired Martlets.

The armada transited the Straits of Gibraltar in the early hours of 10 August 1942 and headed into the Mediterranean to participate in possibly the greatest convoy battle of the war.

During the late afternoon of the 10th, a Vichy-French civilian flying-boat en route to Algeria flew over the fleet, and although allowed to pass unhindered, it radioed a sighting, which was of course picked up by the Germans. Following the French sighting, at dawn the next day the first enemy reconnaissance aircraft was detected and it duly sent off its report before escaping. The location reports had allowed submarine patrols to position themselves, and shortly after midday, as *Furious* prepared to fly off its Spitfires, U-73 hit HMS *Eagle* with four torpedoes and it went down in six minutes. Four of the vessel's precious Hurricanes, from 801 NAS, were airborne at the time, and three landed on *Victorious* and the other on *Indomitable*.

With the enemy fully alerted as to the convoy's position, further attacks were expected, although with its task achieved, *Furious* and its escorts returned to Gibraltar.

The following morning – 12 August – one of 1(F)./122's Ju 88Ds regained contact around 0600 hrs. It was the start of a very long day for the convoy defences. The first engagements were made soon after 0700 hrs when Fulmars of 884 NAS, led by Lt Churchill, sent a Z.1007bis into the sea in flames. Two hours later, Hurricanes of 800 and 880 NASs from *Indomitable*, backed up by three more Sea Hurricanes and four Fulmars from *Victorious*, were directed to the north-east to intercept an incoming raid by two-dozen Ju 88s.

Lt 'Moose' Martyn's section engaged a pair of Ju 88s, with Martyn himself hitting the starboard engine of one that was in turn attacked by Sub Lt Hastings, whose fire caused it to spiral into the sea. This shared

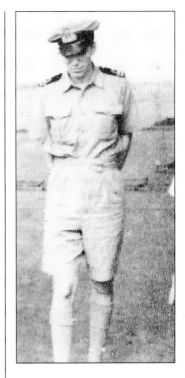

Lt 'Moose' Martyn, who made his first claims over Norway in 1940, became an ace flying Sea Hurricanes on 12 August 1942 during the *Pedestal* convoy, when he shot down a Ju 88 and shared in the destruction of a second bomber (*Owen Dinsdale*)

Powering up on *Indomitable*, Sea Hurricane AF955/7-E of 880 NAS was the regular aircraft of Lt Dickie Cork, who first flew it on 25 October 1941. He used it to attack Vichy-French gun positions during the landings at Diego Suarez on 6 May 1942 (*Owen Dinsdale*)

victory saw Martyn become the first of several Royal Navy pilots to 'make ace' that day.

More Hurricanes under the leadership of the charismatic Lt Cdr Bill Bruen of 800 NAS then entered the fray, and he destroyed a Ju 88 and hit another. As this attack ended, fighters from 880 NAS, led by Cork, arrived. Afterwards, in a press interview, he described the scene;

'The sky at first sight seemed filled with aircraft. The enemy kept in tight formation and our fighters snapped at their heels, forcing them to break in all directions. One Junkers turned away from the main group and I led my section down towards it. I was well ahead and fired when it filled my sights. Smoke poured from its wings and it disappeared below me into the sea. A few minutes later I saw another Ju 88 out of the corner of my eye heading along the coast of North Africa, so I set off in pursuit by myself. At 1000 ft I came within range and fired. It seemed to stagger in the air, then dropped into the sea with a big splash.'

Later in the morning torpedo-bombers from the *Regia Aeronautica* and German Ju 88s from Sicily approached. Hurricanes of 801 NAS, led by Lt Cdr Brabner, were up, and with Lt 'Sloppy' Johnston of 806 NAS heading four Martlets, they countered the raid. Also in the air were Fulmars from *Victorious,* led by 884 NAS CO 'Buster' Hallett.

As the raid built further, Sea Hurricanes led by Lt Cdr Bill Bruen were scrambled from *Indomitable.* It was the Fulmars that attacked first, as the Ju 88s, having dropped their special 'motor bombs', turned for home. Three were reportedly seen falling in flames, with the crews baling out, and a fourth left the area trailing smoke – all were credited to Hallett and Lt Frank Pennington, so making the former the Navy's second ace of the day. Rupert Brabner's Hurricanes then attacked the approaching S.84

Sea Hurricanes from 800 NAS prepare for launch as *Indomitable* approaches Gibraltar following its participation in the *Pedestal* operation. The aircraft nearest to the camera is P5206, which Sub Lt Andy Thomson used to shoot down a Ju 87 and a Bf 109 on 12 August 1942. Behind is Z4550 in which his CO, Lt Cdr Bill Bruen, shot down two bombers and shared a third with Thomson that same day (*R S G Mackay*)

The most successful Royal Navy pilot on the Martlet was Sub Lt John Cotching, who made his first claims during *Pedestal*. He is seen here taxiing forward on *Indomitable* in AM968, in which he made his first claims on 12 August – an S.79 and an Re.2001 shot down (*via B Cull*)

Sea Hurricane AF974/7-D of 880 NAS is positioned on *Indomitable's* forward lift in 1942. The fighter was active during the *Pedestal* convoy battle when Sub Lt Brownlee damaged a Ju 88. Forward of this aircraft near the left bow is BD721/ 7-Z, which was flown several times by Lt Cork (*Owen Dinsdale*)

torpedo-bombers, their attack coinciding with that of Johnston's Martlets. Brabner hit two that were credited to him as destroyed – not only was he the third naval pilot to become an ace during the day, but also the first sitting Member of Parliament to do so! Others pilots claimed too, including Martlet pilot Sub Lt John Cotching, who destroyed an S.79. Then Bruen's section from 800 NAS arrived, and he claimed another S.84 destroyed in concert with Sub Lt Andy Thomson, who also attacked an S.79 which then crashed into the sea – he made two further claims later in the day.

Elsewhere, others too were fighting desperately, and despite these successes, some of the enemy bombers had got through. As they left, Lt Johnston attacked a Ju 88 that he reported over the radio had crashed, before he then headed back to *Indomitable*. One of the ship's officers described the next few tragic minutes;

'From a sky smeared with the dispersing gunfire smoke, a lone Martlet came in low and too fast. Its hook caught a wire, but this was torn out of the fuselage and the aeroplane slewed out over the catwalk, a few feet in

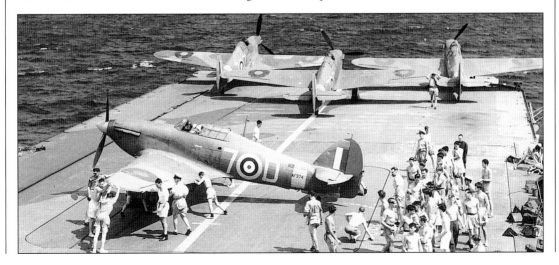

front of me. As though in slow motion, I watched the pilot, Lt Johnston, try to climb out of the cockpit, but the aeroplane turned on its back and fell into the sea. He had been wounded in one of the many air battles. I felt numb.'

'Sloppy' Johnston was not the only CO lost, as 880 NAS's Lt Cdr 'Butch' Judd was killed attacking a formation of He 111s. Dickie Cork duly assumed command of the unit.

After some further engagements, there then followed something of a hiatus before attacks resumed in the late afternoon. Once again Italian-flown Ju 87Rs, with a large escort of

C.202 fighters, made an appearance, as did various Luftwaffe bombers from Pantelleria, protected by Bf 109s. The standing patrols were initially vectored to intercept the approaching aircraft, and other fighters were hastily launched, including one flown by John Cotching, who shot down an Re.2001 fighter of 362ª *Squadriglia*. The Royal Navy fighters were then ordered to clear the area due to their proximity to the fleet barrage, and eventually they were vectored onto new threats. During his interview, Cork recalled;

'I counted ten following their usual tactic of flying close to the sea in a tight group, but one lagged behind and I picked him off and he crashed beside a group of destroyers, which then opened fire on me!'

Cork scored further victories during the evening, and his final kill made him the only Royal Navy pilot of the war to claim five destroyed in a day. He subsequently received the DSO for his exploits.

Unfortunately, just as *Indomitable* launched its last section of Sea Hurricanes, a dozen German-flown Ju 87s began their dives and struck

One of the Royal Navy's most successful fighter pilots, and the only one to claim five aircraft destroyed in a day, Lt Dickie Cork of 880 NAS is seen here sat in the cockpit of his Sea Hurricane soon after *Pedestal* (*Tim Graves*)

With *Eagle* and *Victorious* ahead, Sea Hurricanes of 800 NAS are prepared for launch from *Indomitable* as they shepherd the vital merchant ships towards Malta during *Pedestal*. The nearest aircraft was used by Sub Lt Roberts to shoot down a Ju 88 on 12 August, although he was then forced to ditch, but was safely recovered (*Owen Dinsdale*)

the carrier with two direct hits and three near misses. One of the last aircraft launched was flown by young Scot Sub Lt Blythe Ritchie of 800 NAS, and he fired on one of the Stukas as it pulled out of its dive. He saw the cockpit cover fly off just prior to the aircraft flying into the sea. Five minutes later Ritchie latched onto another Ju 87, as he later described;

'I saw one Ju 87 at 400 ft and chased it for approximately a mile. I did a beam attack at 100 yards and saw part of the cowling fly off, then flew around to its stern and closed to 60 yards, where I saw the gunner double up. It was now smoking and on fire on the starboard side. The starboard wing dropped and it went into the sea from 200 ft.'

Ritchie later shot down a third Stuka, setting him well on the way to becoming an ace.

When the heavy escort turned west soon afterwards, not a single merchant ship had been lost. However, with its organic air cover gone, the *Pedestal* convoy was to suffer grievous losses before reaching land-based air cover. Nevertheless, sufficient materiel reached the island to ensure its survival. It had been an epic struggle, and possibly the finest hour for the Fleet Air Arm's fighters.

THE *TORCH* LANDINGS

The Battle of El Alamein, fought in October 1942, had dramatically changed the Allied situation in Egypt, and in an effort to hasten the end of the campaign extensive amphibious landings were planned for French North Africa, code named Operation *Torch*. Air cover would initially be provided from British and American carriers and, to give the impression of a US only operation, and thus possibly reduce the level of Vichy-French reaction, all carrier aircraft wore US markings. The large force sailed from the UK in mid October, but Malta still needed reinforcement,

For Operation *Torch*, the Seafires of 801 NAS embarked in *Furious* wore US stars. The squadron was led by ace Lt Bob Macdonald-Hall, seen here standing on the extreme right with a 'full set' beard. He was also credited with the Seafire's first combat claim – a Ju 88 damaged (*P J Hutton via C F Shores*)

A smiling Lt Denis Jeram of 888 NAS heads off the deck after landing back on *Formidable*, possibly after he had just claimed his fifth victory on 6 November 1942 in the days prior to *Torch* (*Author's Collection*)

Martlet IV FN112 of 888 NAS prepares to launch from *Formidable* off Algeria. It is believed that Denis Jeram was flying this aircraft when he claimed his fifth victory on 6 November 1942. A few days later, in the hands of another pilot, it also shot down an He 111 (*via R C Sturtivant*)

so HMS *Furious* disembarked most of its Seafires (from 801 and 807 NASs) so as to allow yet another Spitfire ferry mission – Operation *Train* – to take place.

Returning to Gibraltar, a Ju 88 attacked the ship just as a pair of 801 NAS Seafires were landing. Lt MacDonald-Hall immediately gave chase, but as his cumbersome slipper fuel tank would not jettison, he could get no closer than 300 yards. He was still able to score some hits on the bomber's fuselage, however, thus giving Bob MacDonald-Hall his final claim and the Seafire its combat debut.

As well as *Furious* and the fleet carriers *Formidable* and *Victorious*, a number of escort carriers also participated in *Torch*. On 6 November, shortly after the invasion fleet had sailed through the Straits of Gibraltar for Algeria, Lt Denis Jeram, flying a Martlet from 888 NAS on a CAP from *Formidable*, was ordered to intercept a Vichy reconnaissance aircraft. He attacked what he thought was a Potez Po 63 (actually a Bloch MB.174) off Cap Khamis, in Algeria, at 10,000 ft, and sent it down to claim his fifth kill – this was his first whilst flying a naval aircraft, however.

On the morning of the landings (8 November), 800 NAS from *Biter* was briefed to provide close escort for the first strike on Oran. The unit arrived over the target at dawn and aircraft initially identified as Seafires approached. However, they were Vichy Dewoitine D.520s, and a dogfight ensued. Lt Mike Crosley recounted;

'By pulling hard on the stick I was able to out turn the chap shooting at me, and after two more complete turns, I was beautifully on his tail. After no more than a touch on the button I saw yellow flames coming from his exhausts and almost immediately I saw the pilot climb out of the cockpit and fall away. The D.520 dived straight in and that was that.'

He then closed on another that was chasing a Hurricane, and with a half-second burst sent it down too. Being short on fuel, Crosley recovered aboard HMS *Dasher*. Meanwhile, his CO, Lt Cdr Bill Bruen, had also brought down a D.520 for his ninth, and final kill, whilst Sub Lt 'Jock' Ritchie got another for his fourth victory. However, the Sea Hurricanes of 804 and 891 NASs from *Dasher* had a torrid time. 804 NAS was led by ace Lt Cdr Jackie Sewell, but both units were only partially worked up, and many pilots force-landed on the coast.

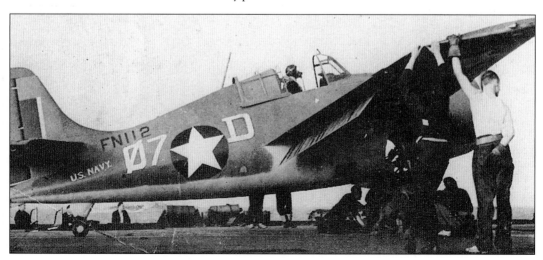

Off Oran, Sub Lt Long, in a Seafire from *Formidable's* 885 NAS, attacked a Vichy Martin 167 over Mers el Kebir harbour and it was last seen low over the sea on fire. A little while later Sub Lt George Baldwin of 807 NAS shot down a D.520 of III/GC 3 flown by Sgt Albert Causse, as he related to the author;

'It was one of the very elegant Dewoitine fighters the French flew, and I can recall its very bright markings. We engaged in a bit of a tussle and eventually I got him in my sights, but my cannon refused to fire. Fortunately, I was able to close sufficiently to use my machine guns.'

There were further encounters with both Vichy fighters and German bombers, one being attacked on the 9th by a pair of Martlets of 888 NAS flown by Lt Denis Jeram and Sub Lt Astin, who soon after 1400 hrs shot down a Ju 88 from which the crew baled out. This was Jeram's final claim.

Naval fighters patrolled the area until land-based fighter cover was established at captured airfields. The carriers were withdrawn on the 13th, but two days later the escort carrier HMS *Avenger* was sunk by a U-boat with massive loss of life. The air group went down with the ship, including the unfortunate 802 NAS, which was sunk for the third time.

With land bases available and Malta eventually secured, the need for carriers in the still dangerous Mediterranean reduced as 1943 progressed. For the invasion of Sicily, *Formidable* and *Indomitable* were positioned to counter any interference by the Italian fleet. However, on the night of 15 July a Ju 88 torpedoed *Indomitable*, causing severe damage.

Two months later, for the landings at Salerno, *Formidable* and *Illustrious* were again positioned to counter any moves by the Italian fleet. Fighter cover over the beaches was provided by the Seafires aboard the five escort carriers of Force 'V', although a combination of the short decks and slack wind led to many deck landing accidents. There were only occasional encounters with sporadic Luftwaffe raids, and on 10 September 1943 897 NAS CO Lt Cdr W C 'Bill' Simpson, flying from HMS *Unicorn*, destroyed two Bf 109s during a sweep – a rare success.

The following year fighters from the escort carriers of Task Force 88 covered the Allied landings in southern France, which began on 15 August. Once more there was little sign of the Luftwaffe, and eventually the force conducted attacks against isolated enemy garrisons in the Aegean. Gradually withdrawn during the autumn of 1944, the carriers then sailed east for operations off Burma.

One of the Royal Navy's great characters was Lt Cdr Bill Bruen, who was flying this Sea Hurricane (JS355) from the escort carrier HMS *Biter* when he shot down a D.520 over La Senia for his eighth, and last, victory (*J M Bruen via J D R Rawlings*)

The Seafire's first confirmed victory was a D.520 shot down by Lt George Baldwin of 807 NAS over La Senia airfield early on 8 November 1942 (*G C Baldwin*)

ATLANTIC AND ARCTIC ACTION

The Norway campaign of 1940 highlighted the need for carrier-capable fighters of much greater performance, which in turn led to a sea-going variant of the Hurricane being developed. Other fighters also found their way into Royal Navy service, with the most significant of these being the tubby Grumman Martlet. Purpose built for naval operations, the first examples of the American fighter came from French contracts that had not been fulfilled prior to the country's invasion by Germany.

These aircraft first saw action on Christmas Day 1940 when a pair from 804 NAS shot down a Ju 88 over Orkney. When formed in January 1941, 880 NAS was also intended to have Martlets, and one of its pilots was Battle of Britain ace Sub Lt Dickie Cork. However, the unit had received just three Martlets when they were withdrawn, pending delivery of the first Sea Hurricanes.

Although the focus of naval fighter operations had moved to the Mediterranean by early 1941, there remained a real need for aircraft carriers with the Home Fleet to counter the threat posed to Atlantic shipping by surface raiders and U-boats. The fall of France also produced an unexpected air threat to trade routes in the elegant shape of the Focke-Wulf Fw 200 Condor, which sank a considerable number of ship – especially vessels sailing alone.

The chronic shortage of carriers led to the development of small escort vessels, but these were still some way off. A short term solution to the problem was the creation of the catapult fighter, whereby an aircraft was mounted on a catapult fitted to the bow of a merchant ship. The fighters flown from these vessels, which were dubbed CAM ships, were manned by the RAF. In May 1941 804 NAS changed its role to provide fighters for the Royal Navy equivalent, known as Fighter Catapult Ships – HM Ships *Ariguani*, *Maplin*, *Springbank* and *Michael E.* These patrolled the areas vulnerable to Condor attack, although the

The Martlet had its first success when the nearest aircraft (BJ562) was used by Lt R H P Carver of 804 NAS to help shoot down a Ju 88 over Orkney on Christmas Day 1940 (*R H P Carver*)

The Martlet's first victim was Leutnant Schipp's Ju 88A 4N+AL of 3(F)./122, which crash-landed at Sandvik (*R H P Carver*)

Martlet III AX824 was one of three that briefly served with 880 NAS before being replaced by Sea Hurricanes. This aircraft was flown on 1 February 1941 by Lt Dickie Cork (*R H P Carver*)

During the summer of 1941 the Fulmars of 809 NAS embarked in HMS *Victorious* and took part in the attack on Kirkenes, in the Arctic (*via J D R Rawlings*)

latter two vessels were sunk. 804 NAS maintained the catapult task for a year, using a mixed force of Sea Hurricanes and Fulmars, but success initially evaded the unit.

However, in the early afternoon of 3 August 1941, HMS *Maplin* was escorting a convoy from Gibraltar when an Fw 200 was sighted. Six minutes later, Sea Hurricane W9277, with Lt Bob Everett at the controls was launched. He subsequently described what happened;

'I intercepted the aircraft after nine minutes' flying, and ranged up alongside it, slightly above, at 600 yards. The Focke-Wulf turned sharply to port, but then seemed to change its mind and turned back onto its original course. By this time I had reached its starboard bow, and three machine guns opened up, as well as the forward cannon. I did a quick turn to port and opened fire. I fired five-second bursts all the way until I was 40 yards astern. Another short burst and my guns were empty. I noticed pieces flying off the starboard side of the Focke-Wulf and it appeared to be alight inside the fuselage. I broke away to port at 30 yards.'

One can only imagine the horror of the German crew at encountering a single seat fighter in mid-Atlantic, and whose fire sent it to destruction. Everett then ditched, was picked up and subsequently received a well deserved DSO. Sadly he was killed in a flying accident in early 1942.

Everett's was not the first Hurricane victory at sea, however, as on 17 July 880 NAS received its first four carrier-capable Sea Hurricanes that were then embarked in HMS *Furious* for the strike on the enemy occupied ports at Petsamo and Kirkenes, in the high Arctic. Lt Dickie Cork flew two defensive patrols, while his CO, Lt Cdr 'Butch' Judd, claimed the Sea Hurricane's first victory when he shot down a Do 18 in

concert with Sub Lt R B Howarth. The other carrier involved was HMS *Victorious*, which had the Fulmars of 809 NAS embarked, and these claimed four victories for the loss of three Fairey fighters.

880 NAS was destined for service aboard the new fleet carrier HMS *Indomitable*, which left the UK in October 1941 to work up in the West Indies. By then the first escort carrier had entered service, HMS *Audacity*, a captured German merchant vessel converted to take a 460-ft long 'flat top', displacing only 10,200 tons and boasting just two arrestor wires and a barrier – and no hangarage!

To support the move of an RAF Hurricane Wing to northern Russia, 802 NAS detached two Martlets to the old carrier HMS *Argus* for its self-defence. The Hurricanes were flown off in the Barents Sea on 7 September, and two days later the Martlets moved onto HMS *Victorious* for operations off Norway. One of the pilots was Sub Lt Jimmy Sleigh, who recalled;

'At about 1400 hrs on 13 September, one of the escort ships signalled that they had spotted a Heinkel approaching. We were steaming in moderate seas with broken cloud cover, and Bertie Williams and I were ordered to take off in our Martlets and intercept. This we did, spotting the He 111 at about 2000 ft on the bearing provided by the escort. I engaged successfully at close range, with the Heinkel returning fire. As I passed over the bomber I felt a jolt and saw the enemy aircraft plunge into the sea. On my way back to the ship, I spotted another Heinkel and proceeded to engage it, with some limited success as I saw the starboard engine burst into flames. On my return to

The Royal Navy's first escort carrier was a converted captured German merchant ship, commissioned as HMS *Audacity*. It embarked the Martlets of 802 NAS, which met with considerable success during the vessel's brief career (*E M Brown*)

The Martlet's first victory when flying from a carrier was claimed by 802 NAS's Sub Lt Jimmy Sleigh whilst he was detached aboard *Victorious* (*J W Sleigh*)

Photographed from a passing Pan Am 'Clipper' flying-boat, the inverted Martlet from 802 NAS is being flown by Sub Lt 'Winkle' Brown. The furthest aircraft, 'Q', is believed to be the one used by Jimmy Sleigh when he claimed his first victory on 13 September 1941 (*E M Brown*)

the ship to refuel, I noticed that the underside of the Wildcat (Martlet) had a gouge down the underside of the fuselage – I must have been very close to the first Heinkel, and was very lucky to escape.'

Sleigh's victory was the first by a Martlet flying from a carrier deck. Soon afterwards they rejoined their squadron in *Audacity* escorting Gibraltar convoys.

From *Audacity,* 802 NAS's first success came on 21 September 1941 when an Fw 200 was shot down by Sub Lts Patterson and Fletcher. There were frequent scrambles, and when found, the enemy return fire was often accurate. On 8 November, for example, another Condor was sighted and the CO and Sub Lt Hutchinson attacked, but Lt Cdr John Wintour, flying BJ516, was shot down and killed. He was swiftly avenged as 'Hutch' then destroyed the Condor. Later that day another Fw 200 was shot down by Sub Lt Eric 'Winkle' Brown. When the ship arrived in Gibraltar, Lt Donald Gibson joined the squadron as its new CO, despite having never previously made a deck landing in a Martlet!

Audacity sailed on 14 December, and the battle around the convoy it was protecting as it headed north was a bitter one. 802 NAS made attacks on both aircraft and U-boats, with Sub Lt Fletcher being shot down by anti-aircraft fire from a submarine that he was strafing. On a more positive note, 'Winkle' Brown brought down his second Condor on the 19th. Later that same day it was Jimmy Sleigh's turn to score a kill, for after a long chase he brought down the fifth Condor from KG 40 to be claimed by the squadron. Two nights later *Audacity* was torpedoed and sunk with much loss of life, although Sleigh and 'Winkle' Brown, who were both awarded the DSC, were among those saved.

With Sea Hurricanes from 802 and 883 NASs embarked, the escort carrier HMS *Avenger* played a pivotal role in the desperate defence of Russia-bound convoy PQ 18 in the Arctic against persistent Luftwaffe attacks in September 1942 (*R S G Mackay*)

—ARCTIC CONVOYS—

Although naval fighter action in the Atlantic was somewhat limited, on the Arctic convoys, German aircraft posed a constant threat to Allied vessels taking war supplies to northern Russia. Flying from bases in northern Norway, *Luftflotte V* fielded more than 150 bombers. After the near destruction of convoy PQ 17 during the summer of 1942, PQ 18, which sailed in early September, had a heavy escort, including the newly built escort carrier HMS *Avenger*. Embarked in the vessel were 12 Sea Hurricanes from 802 NAS, commanded by Lt Ted Taylour, and 883 NAS, led by another successful pilot, Lt Pat Massy.

At lunchtime on the 12th, four Sea Hurricanes drove off a shadowing Bv 138 flying-boat, although the following day, some 150 miles north-west of Bear Island, others arrived and maintained contact. In mid afternoon the first attack developed, which was driven off before a huge formation of Ju 88 and He 111 torpedo-bombers swept towards the convoy. The attack was perfectly timed, for the fighters were still on deck and eight vessels were sunk. Later, four fighters chased an He 115 floatplane, which escaped, but its return fire hit Ted Taylour's aircraft, sending the seven-victory ace down in flames.

The air attacks resumed the next day, with *Avenger* being targeted and its fighters taking a steady toll of the German aircraft attempting to sink the carrier. They shot down at least five bombers, but, more importantly, they broke up the coordination of the attacks, which thus became less effective. Thereafter, the convoy was targeted only sporadically.

Upon his return to England, 883 NAS's CO, Pat Massy, relived the action of 14 September for a press interview, stating;

'You could see them coming in layers, like a wedding cake, and as we took off, it looked as though we had about three aircraft to every layer of "Jerries". Our squadrons had to split up to tackle various bunches of "Huns", and eventually I found myself with my section mate – PO Randle, who was a wizard pilot and a grand fighter – tackling 14 Junkers 88s flying in diamond formation, a pretty hard nut to crack, for if they can keep formation, their crossfire keeps every aeroplane covered.

'However, I made a quarter attack on the leading aeroplane, then swung away straight at one of the aeroplanes on the side of the diamond. At the last second I flicked underneath him – he got the wind up and pulled the nose of his aeroplane hard up, and (*text continues on page 61*)

Aboard *Avenger*, 802 NAS was briefly led by seven-victory ace Lt Ted Taylour until he was shot down by return fire from a shadowing He 115 floatplane that he was attacking on 12 September 1942. His Sea Hurricane fell in flames into the icy Barents Sea (*M Goodman*)

With the battleship HMS *Duke of York* off the bow, Seafire IIC MB257/T of 801 NAS is brought up onto the flightdeck of HMS *Furious* off Norway in July 1943. This aircraft was regularly flown by Lt Peter Hutton, who made seven claims, including 3 1/2 destroyed (*P J Hutton via C F Shores*)

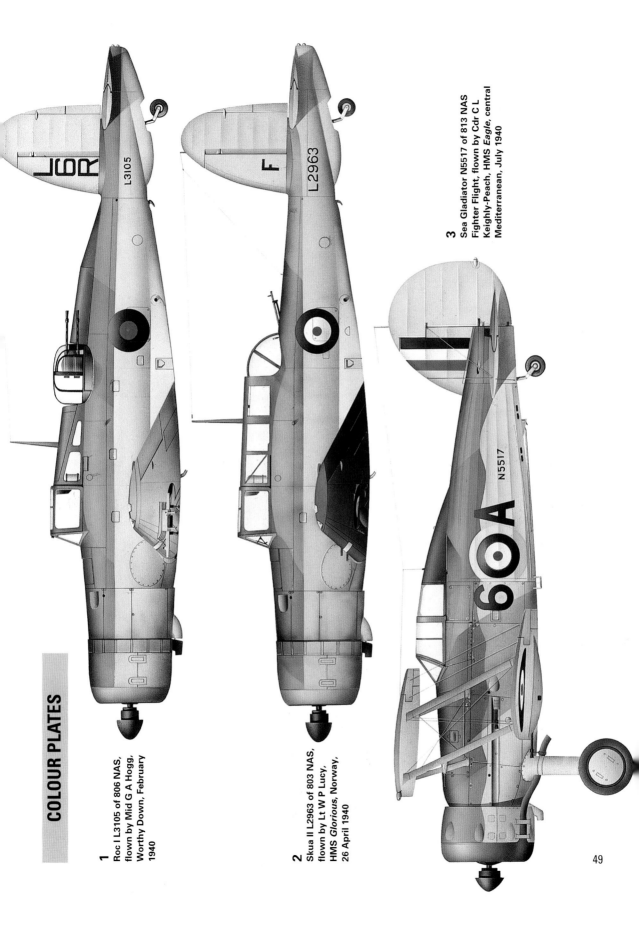

COLOUR PLATES

1
Roc I L3105 of 806 NAS, flown by Mid G A Hogg, Worthy Down, February 1940

2
Skua II L2963 of 803 NAS, flown by Lt W P Lucy, HMS *Glorious*, Norway, 26 April 1940

3
Sea Gladiator N5517 of 813 NAS Fighter Flight, flown by Cdr C L Keighly-Peach, HMS *Eagle*, central Mediterranean, July 1940

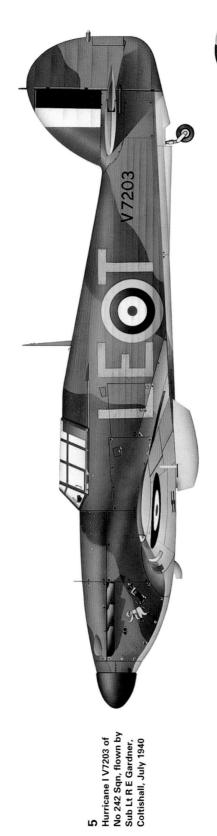

4
Skua II L2927 of
803 NAS, flown by
Lt J M Bruen, HMS *Ark
Royal*, central
Mediterranean, July-
August 1940

5
Hurricane I V7203 of
No 242 Sqn, flown by
Sub Lt R E Gardner,
Coltishall, July 1940

6
Fulmar I N1886 of
806 NAS, flown by
Sub Lt I L F Lowe,
HMS *Illustrious*, off
Malta, 2 September
1940

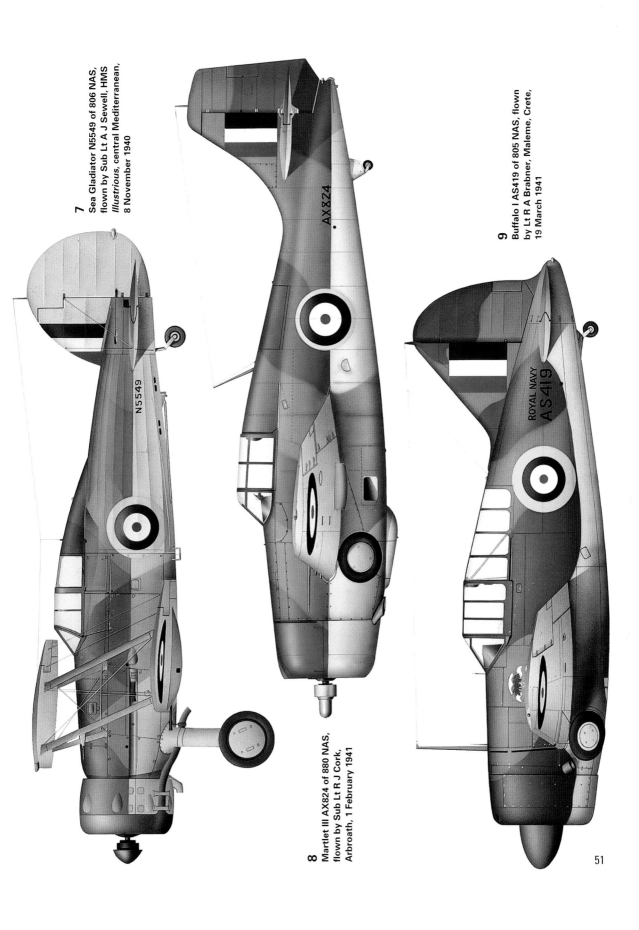

7
Sea Gladiator N5549 of 806 NAS,
flown by Sub Lt A J Sewell, HMS
Illustrious, central Mediterranean,
8 November 1940

8
Martlet III AX824 of 880 NAS,
flown by Sub Lt R J Cork,
Arbroath, 1 February 1941

9
Buffalo I AS419 of 805 NAS, flown
by Lt R A Brabner, Maleme, Crete,
19 March 1941

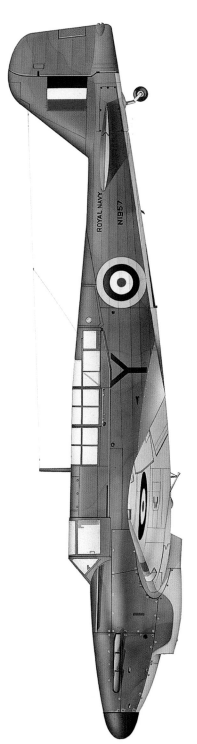

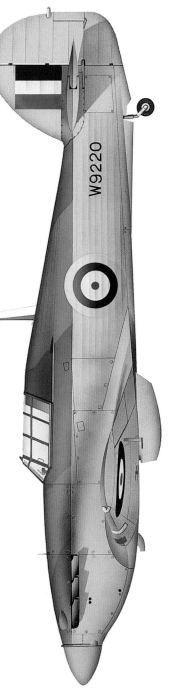

10
Fulmar I N2006 of
803 NAS, flown by
Lt D C E F Gibson,
HMS *Formidable*,
central Mediterranean,
18 April 1941

11
Fulmar I N1957 of 806
NAS, flown by Lt R
MacDonald-Hall, HMS
Formidable, off Crete,
26 May 1941

12
Sea Hurricane IB
W9220 of 880 NAS,
flown by Sub Lt R J
Cork, Arbroath and
St Merryn, March-July
1941

13
Martlet III AM963 of
802B Flt, flown by Sub
Lt J W Sleigh, HMS
Victorious, north
Norway, September
1941

14
Hurricane I Z4932 of
806 NAS/RN Fighter
Squadron, flown by
Sub Lt M F Fell, LG123
Maddelena, Libya,
1 December 1941

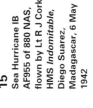

15
Sea Hurricane IB
AF955 of 880 NAS,
flown by Lt R J Cork,
HMS *Indomitable*,
Diego Suarez,
Madagascar, 6 May
1942

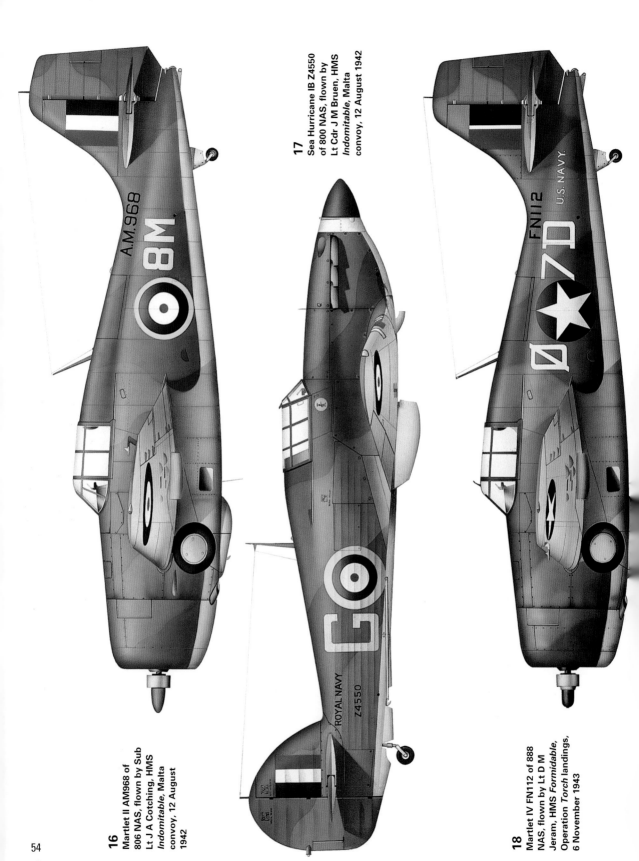

16
Martlet II AM968 of
806 NAS, flown by Sub
Lt J A Cotching, HMS
Indomitable, Malta
convoy, 12 August
1942

17
Sea Hurricane IB Z4550
of 800 NAS, flown by
Lt Cdr J M Bruen, HMS
Indomitable, Malta
convoy, 12 August 1942

18
Martlet IV FN112 of 888
NAS, flown by Lt D M
Jeram, HMS *Formidable*,
Operation *Torch* landings,
6 November 1943

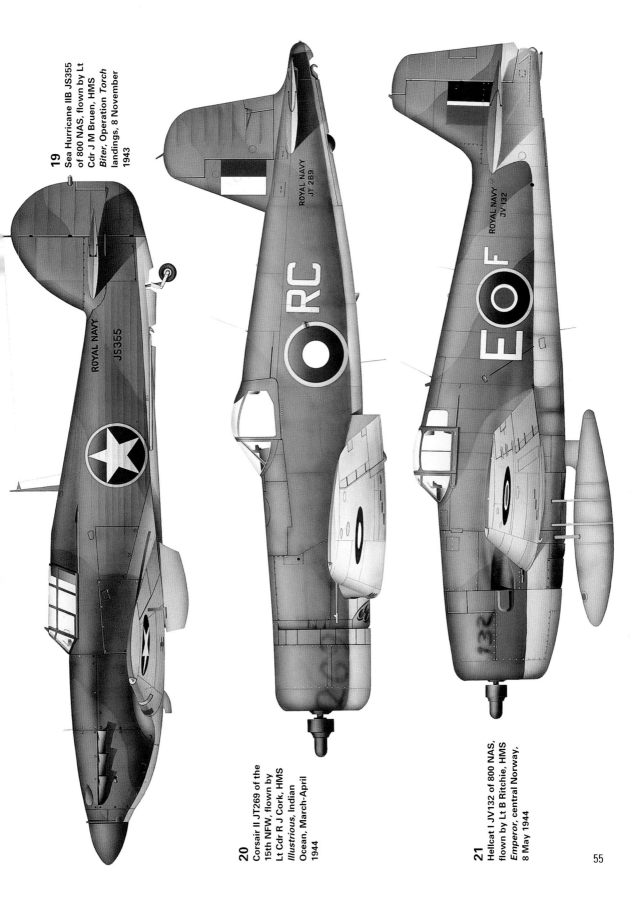

19
Sea Hurricane IIB JS355 of 800 NAS, flown by Lt Cdr J M Bruen, HMS *Biter*, Operation *Torch* landings, 8 November 1943

20
Corsair II JT269 of the 15th NFW, flown by Lt Cdr R J Cork, HMS *Illustrious*, Indian Ocean, March-April 1944

21
Hellcat I JV132 of 800 NAS, flown by Lt B Ritchie, HMS *Emperor*, central Norway, 8 May 1944

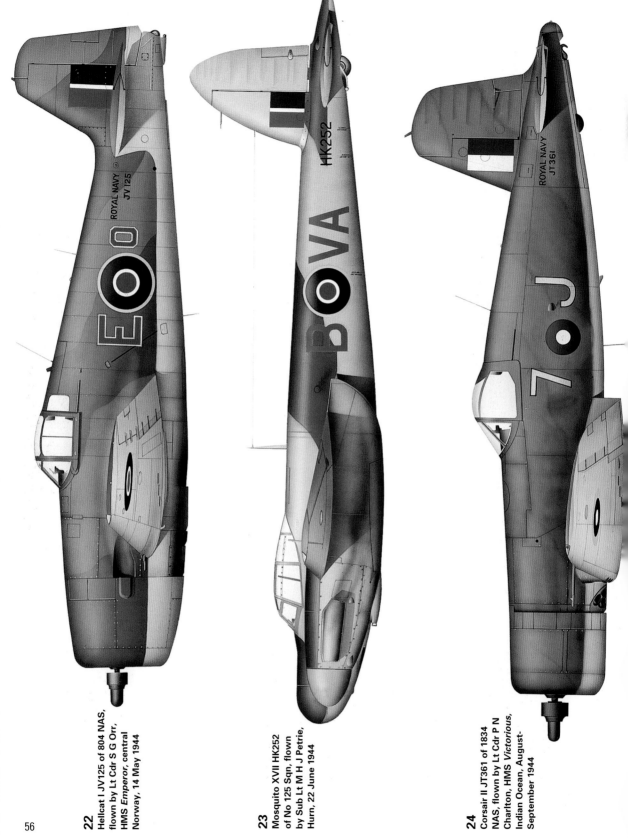

22
Hellcat I JV125 of 804 NAS,
flown by Lt Cdr S G Orr,
HMS *Emperor*, central
Norway, 14 May 1944

23
Mosquito XVII HK252
of No 125 Sqn, flown
by Sub Lt M H J Petrie,
Hurn, 22 June 1944

24
Corsair II JT361 of 1834
NAS, flown by Lt Cdr P N
Charlton, HMS *Victorious*,
Indian Ocean, August-
September 1944

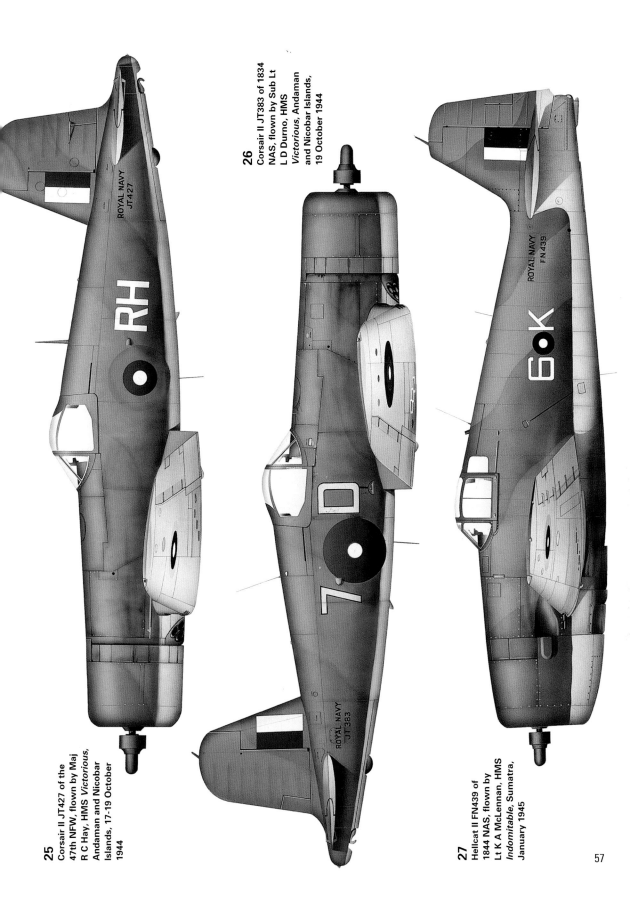

25
Corsair II JT427 of the
47th NFW, flown by Maj
R C Hay, HMS *Victorious*,
Andaman and Nicobar
Islands, 17-19 October
1944

26
Corsair II JT383 of 1834
NAS, flown by Sub Lt
L D Durno, HMS
Victorious, Andaman
and Nicobar Islands,
19 October 1944

27
Hellcat II FN439 of
1844 NAS, flown by
Lt K A McLennan, HMS
Indomitable, Sumatra,
January 1945

57

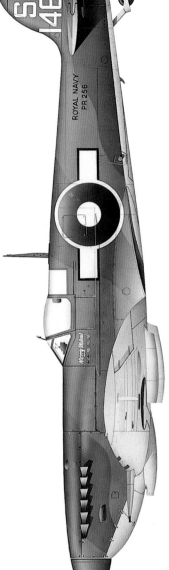

28
Corsair II JT410 of
1836 NAS, flown by
Sub Lt D J Sheppard,
HMS *Victorious*,
Sumatra, January
1945

29
Seafire III PR256 of 894 NAS,
flown by Sub Lt R H
Reynolds, HMS *Indefatigable*,
Okinawa, 1 April 1945

30
Hellcat II JX886 of
1839 NAS, flown by
Sub Lt E T Wilson,
HMS *Indomitable*,
Okinawa, 6 April 1945

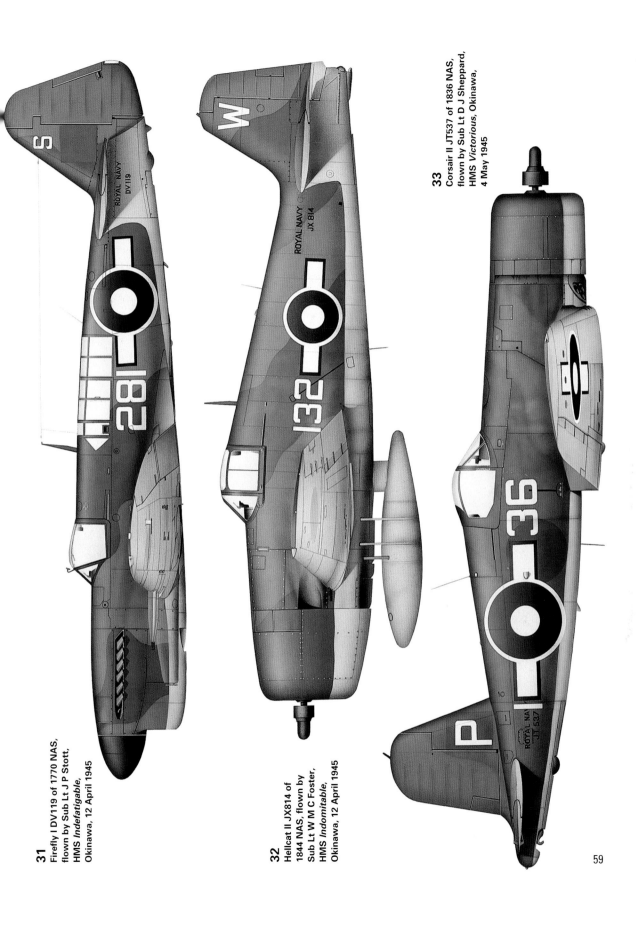

31
Firefly I DV119 of 1770 NAS,
flown by Sub Lt J P Stott,
HMS *Indefatigable*,
Okinawa, 12 April 1945

32
Hellcat II JX814 of
1844 NAS, flown by
Sub Lt W M C Foster,
HMS *Indomitable*,
Okinawa, 12 April 1945

33
Corsair II JT537 of 1836 NAS,
flown by Sub Lt D J Sheppard,
HMS *Victorious*, Okinawa,
4 May 1945

34
Seafire III NN621 of 880 NAS, flown by Lt Cdr R M Crosley, HMS *Implacable*, Japan, August 1945

35
Corsair IV KD658 of 1841 NAS, flown by Lt R H Gray, HMS *Formidable*, Japan, 9 August 1945

36
Seafire III NN300 of 807 NAS/ 4th NFW, flown by Lt Cdr G C Baldwin, HMS *Hunter*, Singapore, September 1945

PO Randle, flying just on my starboard wing, gave him a lovely burst which put paid to his account.

'The formation then broke up, and there was a lovely scrap all over the sky. That sort of thing went on all day. As soon as we were out of ammunition or petrol, we dived down to the carrier, landed, rearmed and refuelled and took off again. My lunch was a gulp of cold tea. Our squadron made 17 sorties that day.'

The action, for which Massy received a DSO, took his total claims to six, including three destroyed, but he tragically died two months later when *Avenger* blew up after a torpedo attack.

Three months before this epic action, the first Seafires had been delivered to 807 NAS. Although a superb interceptor, it did suffer from a limited range and an undercarriage that was much too weak for carrier operations. Nonetheless, the Seafire was a potent type, and also saw service in escort carriers. These vessels usually embarked a composite squadron that comprised a Swordfish flight and a fighter flight, the latter generally using Sea Hurricanes and, later, Martlets (redesignated Wildcats in January 1944).

In July 1943 the Home Fleet mounted Operation *Camera* off Norway, and *Illustrious* embarked 894 NAS's Seafire IICs for the first time. By then the Fleet Air Arm was also starting to receive potent new fighters from the United States, including the Grumman Hellcat. 804 NAS was one of the first units to receive Hellcats, and its CO at the time of its conversion onto the aircraft was 11-victory ace Lt Cdr Stan Orr. He recalled;

'The Hellcat was without a doubt the best, and most popular, naval fighter of the period. It suffered none of the Corsair's stall and visibility problems, being an easy aircraft both to fly and to deck land. It bestowed upon its pilot immense confidence, which was an important thing in those days, as you usually had your hands more than full coping with the enemy!'

THE *TIRPITZ* STRIKES

The brooding menace of the German battleship *Tirpitz* in Scandinavian waters presented the Royal Navy with a constant problem, and required

Lt Cdr Sleigh, in Wildcat V JV429 of 881 NAS, catches the wire on HMS *Pursuer* after a rehearsal sortie for the first strike on *Tirpitz*. He played such a key role in this operation, conducted on 3 April 1944, that he was awarded a DSO. Two months prior to this mission being flown, Sub Lt Brander had shot down an He 177 bomber in JV429 (*J W Sleigh*)

that a substantial carrier force be retained with the Home Fleet to conduct regular operations along the Norwegian coast to cover Russia-bound convoys. During these operations there were occasional brushes with enemy aircraft, but fighter engagements were rare. However, on 9 February 1944 Seafires of 801 NAS from *Furious* had a brisk five-minute combat in which a solitary Bf 109 was destroyed by Lt Wilkinson, although a Seafire was also lost.

At the end of March the fleet sailed to attack the *Tirpitz* in Altenfjord, Norway, the main strike force for Operation *Tungsten* being embarked in *Furious* and *Victorious*. The former also carried the Seafires of 801 and 880 NASs, the latter led by Lt Cdr 'Moose' Martyn, while in *Victorious* the Corsairs of 1834 and 1836 NASs were making the type's combat debut in British service. Additional fighters were embarked in the escort carriers *Pursuer* and *Searcher*, with each vessel boasting four squadrons of Wildcats, while *Emperor* had Hellcat-equipped 800 and 804 NASs.

Just after 0400 hrs on 3 April, when some 120 miles off the Norwegian coast, the first Corsairs of Lt Cdr Noel Charlton's 1834 NAS left *Victorious* and headed for Kaa Fjord in a clear, cold sky. An hour later, the Barracudas began their dives, and one of the Corsair pilots from 1836 NAS who would later make a name for himself in the Pacific was Sub Lt Don Sheppard. He recalled;

'The first strike caught the Germans with their trousers down. We stooged around in high cover at 12,000 ft, from where I counted hit after hit – a dozen perhaps, or more. The *Tirpitz*? It was smoking and burning – just taking it.'

The battleship was hit by 15 bombs and suffered serious internal damage. Whilst the dive-bombers attacked the capital ship, the fighters strafed nearby flak positions and even *Tirpitz* itself.

As this strike left the target area, a second one launched. Again, the follow-up force included Corsair, Wildcat and Hellcat escorts, with one of the latter being flown by Lt Cdr Stan Orr. He remembered;

'Upon arrival over *Tirpitz*, it was found that the smoke screen generated by the Germans had ridden half way up the mountains on either side of Kaafjord. Each flight attacked their pre-briefed gun sites once it was clear that no enemy fighters were in the area. The Hellcat proved itself to be an excellent gunnery platform on this mission.'

Tungsten had been the largest air strike yet undertaken by the Fleet Air Arm, and it was deemed to have been a great success. Later in the month the carrier force attacked enemy shipping in the Bodo and Vestefjord areas, although bad weather interfered with operations somewhat. However, soon after 0800 hrs on 6 May, south west of Kristiansund, 882 NAS Wildcat Vs of Lt John Cotching's section, up from HMS *Searcher*, intercepted a Bv 138 flying-boat and shot it down in flames into the sea.

Ten minutes later Cotching shared in the destruction of a second Bv 138 with three other pilots. These proved to be his final victories, for two days later Cotching's aircraft was hit by flak during an attack on a German coastal convoy. The Grumman fighter flew straight into the sea, carrying the Royal Navy's most successful Martlet/Wildcat pilot to his death. Ironically, shortly afterwards the award of a DSC for Cotching's efforts during the *Tirpitz* attack was announced.

One of the Royal Navy's most successful aces was Lt Cdr Stan Orr, who made his final claims flying Hellcats with 804 NAS during operations off Norway in the late spring of 1944 (*S G Orr*)

That same day – 8 May – Hellcats that had found little opportunity to engage the Luftwaffe in aerial combat were attacked near Gossen Island by Bf 109s and Fw 190s of JG 5. Although the enemy fighters had a superior speed, two Messerschmitts and a Focke-Wulf fell to the Hellcat's firepower. The latter was shot down by Lt Blythe Ritchie of 800 NAS, giving him ace status.

Six days later during another sweep, a Hellcat formation from 800 and 804 NASs spotted some He 115 floatplanes low over the sea just off the Norwegian coast, as Lt Cdr Stan Orr recalled;

'On 14 May both Hellcat squadrons launched nine aircraft apiece as part of *Potluck Able* – a strike against enemy shipping off Rorvik. I led the formation in a climb to 5000 ft following landfall near Vikten Island.'

He then led an attack on some ships, but his attention soon shifted to aircraft that had been spotted flying nearby just above the sea;

'Whilst all this was going on, 800 NAS's flight of four Hellcats had sighted five He 115 floatplanes, whose pilots quickly realised they stood little chance against the marauding Grummans and tried to alight on the water. Two Heinkels were shot down on the first pass – one fell to the guns of "White Flight" leader, Lt Blythe Ritchie – and the remainder made panic landings north of Rorvik. Having successfully bombed our targets, I led "Red Flight" into the fight with the Heinkels, and I believe I made one pass at Ritchie's He 115 just prior to it crash-landing.

'By the time we had knocked our speed off and turned around to run in at them again, the three remaining floatplanes were bobbing up and down on the water like sitting ducks. "White Flight" had since exhausted its ammunition after strafing the remaining He 115s, and it was left to us to finish them off. I shared the sinking of one and then set another alight.'

Hellcats are prepared for action off Norway on the deck of HMS *Emperor* on 14 May 1944. The aircraft on the right is JV105/E-W of 804 NAS, while immediately behind it is JV132/E-F, which was flown that day by Lt Blythe Ritchie of 800 NAS. The seven-kill ace scored his final 1 1/2 victories on the 14th when he shot down an He 115 and shared in the destruction of a second Heinkel floatplane with Lt Cdr Stan Orr. Six days earlier, whilst again flying JV132, Ritchie had destroyed an Fw 190 to become an ace. His Hellcat also has its number crudely painted on its nose. Ritchie was killed on active duty just a matter of weeks later (*S G Orr*)

3rd NFW air gunnery instructor Lt Mike Crosley shot down a Bf 109 on 7 June 1944 near the D-Day beachhead to become an ace (*HQ No 34 Wing records*)

In early June 1944, Seafire pilots of the 3rd NFW fought a number of air combats over Normandy whilst they were bombardment spotting. NF547/2D of 885 NAS damaged two Bf 109s when flown by Sub Lt Hales on D-Day, while Sub Lt Chamen used it to shoot down a Bf 109 near Caen two days later (*H Neilson*)

Orr was credited with a shared victory – these were also the last that Royal Navy Hellcats claimed against the Luftwaffe. Soon afterwards *Victorious* left the Home Fleet and sailed for the Indian Ocean.

Convoy escort operations continued well into 1944, and these claimed occasional successes over German shadowers. On 25 May Sea Hurricanes of 835 NAS, embarked in HMS *Nairana*, shot down a huge Ju 290 maritime reconnaissance aircraft into the Bay of Biscay, and the following day Sub Lts Sam Mearns and Frank Wallis destroyed another from 1./FAG 5. The latter machine, flown by Lt Kurt Nonneberg, was the last aircraft to fall to the Sea Hurricane, and the squadron exchanged its veteran Hawker fighters for Wildcats several months later.

D-DAY SUPPORT

During the planning of the invasion of France, code named Operation *Overlord*, most of the fire support for the landing forces on the days immediately following D-Day would be provided by bombardment from Allied warships cruising off the Normandy coast. These vessels would require accurate airborne spotting for their guns, and this was clearly a naval task. In order to ensure the correct levels of coordination between ships and spotting aircraft during *Overlord*, the 3rd Naval Fighter Wing (NFW) – 808, 885 and 886 NASs, flying Seafires, and 897 NAS, equipped with Spitfire Vs – formed the Air Spotting Pool at Lee-on-Solent. RAF units and the US Navy's VCS-7, all using Spitfires, were also assigned to the Royal Navy-controlled pool.

No 3 NFW was led by six-victory ace Lt Cdr 'Buster' Hallett, and he had several other notable pilots within his command. One such individual was 23-year-old Lt Mike Crosley, who was the wing's Air Gunnery Instructor. Having flown three missions unopposed on D-Day, Crosley finally encountered the enemy during his second sortie on 7 June. He initially chased a Bf 109, which he lost, but he soon made up for it when he spotted another German fighter;

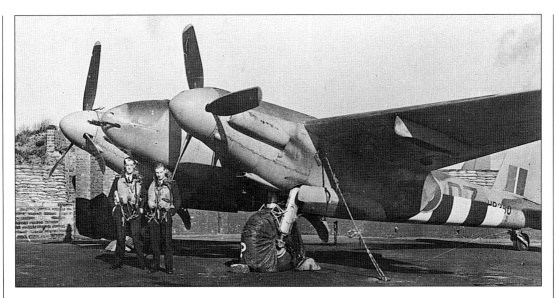

'I climbed up to 7000 ft, having lost my No 2 in the chase, and hardly am I there but I see another Messerschmitt (it might have been the same one) about six miles away, doing the same thing. I know he is a "Hun", so I get in close, out of the sun, and let him have it from 200 yards to mighty close. He goes down through a cloud streaming smoke and glycol and comes out in a vertical spiral dive, hitting the deck in a bright orange flash. What a life!'

Thus did the youthful Crosley become the latest Royal Navy pilot to become an ace.

The wing also had further successes during the *Overlord* period, when Sub Lt Barraclough of 897 NAS shot down a Bf 109 and Sub Lt Sam Lang of 886 NAS destroyed an Fw 190, although he was then hit by another and forced down – he was duly picked up by nearby Commandos. Enemy fighters also claimed Lang's CO. The wing's losses were quite severe, mainly due to the enemy's vicious light flak, although just prior to it being withdrawn 885 NAS's Sub Lt Chamen of the South African Naval Force (SANF) shot down a Bf 109 near Caen.

Other Royal Navy fighter pilots were operating over the beachhead in June 1944, as a number of them had been seconded to RAF Mosquito nightfighter squadrons in order to gain experience in the role, pending the development of similar aircraft for shipboard operations. Several of these individuals claimed victories, including New Zealander Sub Lt Malcolm Petrie who, with his observer, Lt F A Noyes, served with No 125 Sqn at Hurn, on the south coast. On the night of 22 June, off the coast at Fecamp, north of Le Havre, they engaged and shot down two Ju 88s attempting to attack vulnerable offshore shipping.

Fellow New Zealanders Lts J A Cramp and J H B Maggs of No 151 Sqn also got a kill during an intruder mission over central France when they shot down a Do 24 flying-boat.

Others ranged further afield over occupied Europe, and in mid-evening of 17 September 1944, a Mosquito of No 29 Sqn, flown by Royal Navy crew Lt Douglas Price and Sub Lt Robert Armitage, left Hunsdon to patrol over the Arnhem area, where the British 1st Airborne Division

During 1944, a number of Royal Navy crews flew Mosquitos with RAF nightfighter squadrons, including Lts Cramp and Maggs of No 151 Sqn who, during one intruder sortie, shot down a Do 24 flying-boat and damaged a Bf 108 trainer (*M N Austin*)

The leading Royal Navy nightfighter pilot (with five claims, including three destroyed) was Lt Douglas Price. He and his observer, Sub Lt Bob Armitage, flew Mosquitos with No 29 Sqn between October 1943 and October 1944 (*No 29 Sqn records*)

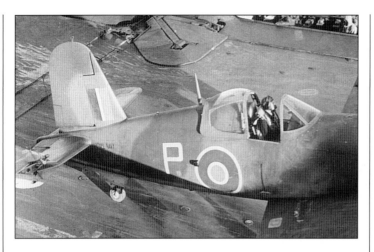

An American type that made its British combat debut during the *Tirpitz* strikes of 1944 was the Corsair, although the aircraft saw no action against the Luftwaffe during these missions because of their designated flak suppression role. JT590 of 1842 NAS bears the scars from one such mission after recovering onto *Formidable* on 22 August (*via R S G Mackay*)

had begun dropping earlier in the day. Price and Armitage already had two victories and two damaged to their names since joining the unit, and some 25 miles from Arnhem, soon after 2300 hrs, they gained a radar contact as Price recalled;

'I was flying at 4500 ft when my navigator obtained a contact at "two o'clock", crossing from right to left, at a distance of four miles, bearing 075. I turned hard to port and the contact was held at "12 o'clock" at four miles. I immediately started to climb hard and followed the aircraft, which took gentle evasive action. I closed the range, my height being 11,500 ft, and obtained a visual on a very bright single exhaust well above and to starboard. I closed range and obtained a silhouette, which was identified as an Me 110 carrying long range tanks slung under the wings, outboard of each engine. My navigator confirmed this identification.

'Just before I obtained visual, the enemy aircraft started to make a hard turn, and throttling hard back, caused the engines to emit a shower of sparks. In spite of this evasion, contact was held. I fired a three-second burst on a very bright white exhaust on the starboard engine, causing it to explode, with debris flying off. The windscreen was covered with oil and its speed fell off considerably. I broke away hard to starboard and noticed that the engine had fallen out of the wing of the aircraft, which dived vertically to the deck with its port engine enveloped in flames.'

The pair had just achieved their final victory, and with a total of five claims, they were the most successful Royal Navy nightfighting team.

Earlier, during July, the Royal Navy had conducted a further strike – code named Operation *Mascot* – on *Tirpitz* from three fleet carriers, with the fighter escort comprising 1841 NAS's Corsairs from *Formidable*, 18 Hellcats of 1840 NAS from *Furious* and, making their operational debut, 1770 NAS's Fireflies from *Indefatigable*, under the command of Maj V B G 'Cheese' Cheesman, Royal Marines, who was awarded the DSO for the determined way he led his squadron. However, no serious damage was done to *Tirpitz*, and the results overall were disappointing.

A final series of strikes by the Fleet Air Arm, code named Operation *Goodwood*, was launched in August 1944. The first two went ahead on the 22nd, with fighter escorts being provided by Corsairs from 1841 and 1842 NASs, 887 NAS's Seafires, 1840 NAS's Hellcats and 1770 NAS's Fireflies. 1841 NAS's Corsairs swept down to strafe the flak defences in

Yet another type to make its combat debut during the *Tirpitz* strikes was the Fairey Firefly, which also flew in the anti-flak role with 1770 NAS from HMS *Indefatigable* (via *G R Pitchfork*)

the face of heavy fire, during which Lt 'Hammy' Gray led his section to attack three enemy destroyers at anchor. Two days later, the heaviest strikes in this series of operations went in, and 1840 NAS CO, Lt Cdr Archie Richardson, from *Indefatigable* was lost. In his report, the C-in-C Home Fleet said;

'His most conspicuous gallantry and inflexible determination to inflict the maximum amount of damage upon the enemy, without any regard to his own safety, resulted during his third attack on the *Tirpitz* in the sacrifice of his life.'

The award of the Victoria Cross was recommended, but that of a posthumous mention in despatches was made instead. On 29 August *Formidable* and *Indefatigable* launched the final strike, although again the results were disappointing.

Flying CAP over the carriers for the first strike were Seafires of 894 NAS, and in the late afternoon Lt Palmer and Sub Lt Reynolds were vectored onto some unidentified contacts off the North Cape. Soon afterwards, in visibility of less than half-a-mile, and with a very low cloud base, the pair spotted a Bv 138 flying-boat. They took turns in attacking the aircraft, and the flying-boat crashed into the sea on fire. Almost immediately they were given a steer onto another contact, and in an almost identical engagement, the pair downed a second Bv 138. These claims set Richard Reynolds on his way to becoming the only Seafire ace.

The build up of carrier strength against Japan saw all fleet carriers sent east, although *Implacable* initially conducted some operations off Norway prior to sailing for the Pacific in March 1945. Escort carriers then continued convoy escorts and coastal strikes off Norway until the end of the war. The last Fleet Air Arm strike in Europe was made on 4 May 1945, although this was not, apparently, the final action. Five days later, following the German surrender, a Ju 88 flown by Oberleutnant Friedrich Droste of II./KG 200 was attacked and badly damaged over the Skagerrak by four fighters from either *Trumpeter* or *Searcher*.

This proved to be the very last aerial combat of the European war.

THE RISING SUN

The Japanese assault against Malaya in December 1941 proved a traumatic experience for the Allies, and the Royal Navy in particular following the early loss of the battleship HMS *Prince of Wales* and battlecruiser HMS *Repulse*. The Fleet Air Arm played only a small part in this campaign, with HMS *Indomitable* mainly being used to ferry RAF fighters to Java.

After the fall of Singapore and the East Indies, Ceylon became the Royal Navy's main base, and in February 1942 two fighter squadrons from the desert, newly re-equipped with Fulmars, moved into Ratmalana, near Colombo. 803 NAS was led by Lt Bruce McEwen, while 806 NAS was under the command of Lt Robert Johnston. Intelligence indicated a probable Japanese naval attack on Ceylon, and in late March HMS *Formidable* disembarked two of 888 NAS's Martlets to China Bay.

At dawn on 5 April (Easter Sunday), 125 Japanese carrier aircraft struck Colombo. Amongst the fighters scrambled were some Fulmars, most getting airborne whilst under attack and two from each squadron were quickly shot down. Lt Mike Hordern of 806 NAS recalled;

'I was on my own, and saw a number of enemy aircraft circling over the sea. I approached through broken cloud cover, at about 5000 ft, and made one pass before breaking off at high speed and seeing an aircraft burning on the surface of the sea. I was credited with one Navy 96 (A6M2 Zero) shot down, seen and confirmed by a naval officer standing outside the Mount Lavinia Hotel.'

The Royal Navy suffered heavy losses, with the cruisers *Cornwall* and *Dorsetshire* both being sunk off the coast of Ceylon, whilst other shipping and facilities were badly hit in Colombo harbour. Also out at sea, HMS *Indomitable* remained unseen by the enemy, and its Sea Hurricanes remained on alert.

The Fulmars of 803 NAS saw action against the Japanese over Ceylon during the devastating series of air strikes made during Easter 1942. Although the big fleet fighters enjoyed some success against their Imperial Japanese Navy counterparts, they also suffered heavy losses (*A V Skeet*)

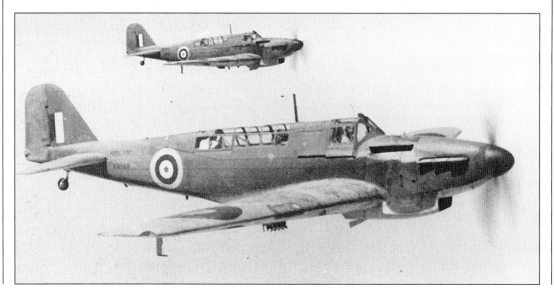

Four days later Vice Admiral Chuichi Nagumo's carriers raided Trincomalee, inflicting heavy damage, including sinking the old carrier HMS *Hermes*. Eight Fulmars from 806 NAS were scrambled (flown single seat), but they arrived in time only to see the carrier going down. The Fulmars then engaged the enemy aircraft in a battle that lasted almost half-an-hour, during which time 806 NAS's CO, Lt Robert 'Sloppy' Johnston, shot down a D3A 'Val' dive-bomber for his first confirmed victory. Sub Lt Barry Nation also claimed a 'Val', whilst a third fell to Sub Lt Paul Peirano, who was one of two pilots subsequently killed.

INTERLUDES

Japanese advances into the Indian Ocean raised the spectre of their occupation of the Vichy-French held island of Madagascar, so the Allies decided that a pre-emptive seizure of the huge natural harbour at Diego Suarez, in the north of the island, was a prudent move. Air cover for the assault, code named Operation *Ironclad*, would initially be provided by the carriers HMS *Indomitable* and the newly repaired *Illustrious*. The former carried a dozen Fulmars of 800 NAS, led by veteran ace Lt Cdr Bill Bruen, and Lt 'Sloppy' Johnston's 806 NAS. Lt Cdr Judd's 880 NAS flew the embarked Sea Hurricanes, and the unit included Battle of Britain ace Lt Dickie Cork within its ranks. Aboard *Illustrious* were the Martlets of 881 and 882 NASs.

Ironclad began with Commando landings in the early hours of 5 May 1942, and at dawn Martlets attacked Arrachart airfield and hit the hangars, destroying a number of Vichy aircraft. 880 NAS's task was to cover the town, harbour and Antsirane airfield, where the Vichy squadrons were based. Although he disliked publicity, Dickie Cork later described the attack for a press interview;

'Voices crackled over the R/T, and above the din the CO could be heard cursing and swearing as he always did. A large hangar dominated the aerodrome, and we could see a number of aircraft inside – we raked the building, and its contents, with our gunfire. Pulling away, I spotted two monoplanes to one side, banked to bring them into my sights and fired a three-second burst, hitting both "midships". All in all a job well done, and a good raid in which to "blood" some of the newer men.'

The following day, with troops ashore encountering heavy resistance, air cover was provided by Martlets from 881 NAS. During the course of the mission, the Royal Navy pilots spotted three Potez Po.63-11 bombers over the town. Lt Ronald Bird and Sub Lt John Waller went after one, with the former's first burst killing the rear gunner. The Potez was soon on fire, although its pilot gallantly remained at his controls, allowing the observer to bale out. A second Potez then fell to Lt Chris Tompkinson.

The stubborn Vichy-French resistance was finally broken on the 7th, while above the battle 881 NAS's Martlets engaged three Vichy Morane MS.406 fighters. As the Martlets dived, Cne Leonetti hit the leading one, which force-landed. The Martlets' top cover then intervened, and Tompkinson sent one of the Moranes down for his second victory in successive days. His No 2, Sub Lt John Waller, also shot a Morane down, before combining with Sub Lt Lyon to destroy the third fighter in what proved to be the last aerial engagement of the operation, as the Vichy-French surrendered soon afterwards.

During early 1943, HMS *Victorious* was attached to the US Pacific Fleet. One of its Martlet squadrons was 882 NAS, commanded by ace Lt Ivan Lowe. He is seen here (on the right) meeting Prime Minister Winston Churchill on the eve of the ship departing home waters for the Pacific (*G F Peat*)

Illustrious returned to Madagascar in September with 806 and 881 NASs embarked to support the capture of the remainder of the island, but there was no air combat.

In early 1943 HMS *Victorious* was detached for service with the US Navy due to the critical shortage of American aircraft carriers following the battles of 1942. Initially, there was a period of training during which the crew of *Victorious* familiarised themselves with the US Navy's operational procedures, before sailing to join the Pacific Fleet at Pearl Harbor. When the vessel began frontline operations on 7 May 1943, its air group included three fighter squadrons with Martlet IVs – 882 NAS, under Lt Cdr F A Shaw, 896 NAS, led by Lt Cdr Barry Nation, and 898 NAS, commanded by six-victory ace Lt Cdr Ivan Lowe.

Victorious joined up with USS *Saratoga*, and in June they covered the US landing on New Georgia, in the Solomon Islands, and then briefly operated in the Coral Sea. However, with the arrival of new US carriers in-theatre shortly afterwards, *Victorious* and its squadrons were released back to the Home Fleet after six months away. To the frustration of all, its squadrons had seen no action against the Japanese whilst in the Pacific.

INDIAN OCEAN STRIKES

The renaissance of the Eastern Fleet was initially based around HMS *Illustrious*, which had the first two operational Corsair squadrons (1830

When *Victorious* joined the Eastern Fleet in Ceylon in early 1944, it had the Corsairs of the 15th NFW embarked. The wing was led by Lt Cdr Dickie Cork, who flew this personally marked aircraft (JT269). Sadly, he was killed in a flying accident prior to the 15th NFW seeing action (*Tim Graves*)

The Eastern Fleet carriers saw sporadic action in the Indian Ocean during 1944, including an attack on Sabang in July when *Illustrious* embarked the Corsairs of 1830 and 1833 NASs. The nearest aircraft, JT297 of 1833 NAS, was flown by Lt Munnock when he shot down a Ki-21 bomber during the raid (*Admiralty via R S G Mackay*)

Nicknamed 'Fearless Freddie', 1834 NAS's CO was Lt Cdr Noel Charlton, who had made his first claims over Norway in 1940 and become an ace flying Hurricanes over the desert in 1941 (*Admiralty via R S G Mackay*)

In mid September 1944 Eastern Fleet carriers struck at Sigli, on Sumatra. On return to *Victorious*, the drop tank of Corsair II JT361, flown by Lt Cdr Noel Charlton, released and ignited in spectacular fashion. He was uninjured and the aircraft repaired, but it was subsequently lost in a landing accident on 1 January 1945 whilst being flown by Lt Peter Carmichael, who was to shoot down a MiG-15 in a Sea Fury during the Korean War (*Admiralty via R S G Mackay*)

and 1833 NASs) embarked. In mid April 1944, in company with USS *Saratoga*, *Illustrious'* squadrons mounted a strike on Sabang, off northern Sumatra, as a distant diversion to landings in New Guinea. Another strike, again in company with *Saratoga*, was carried out in May, and then on 21 June *Illustrious'* aircraft attacked Port Blair, in the Andaman Islands, again as a diversion at the request of the Americans.

By then both HMS *Victorious* and HMS *Indomitable* had also joined the Eastern Fleet in the Indian Ocean, with the former having the 47th Naval Fighter Wing (NFW), comprising Corsair-equipped 1834 and 1836 NASs, embarked.

Victorious joined *Illustrious* in another attack on Sabang on 21 July, code named Operation *Crimson*. The ships also embarked additional Corsairs from 1837 and 1838 NASs, and many lessons were learned by the inexperienced aircrews, not the least of which was the need to speed up rendezvousing overhead the carrier after take-off. As the force withdrew, the Japanese mounted an air attack on the carriers, and Sub Lt Ben Heffer of 1837 NAS, who was on deck alert, was launched;

'I was directed towards the enemy at 1645 hrs and sighted five aircraft. There was a large storm astern the fleet, but *Victorious* managed to vector me onto the enemy. A Japanese aircraft dived past me and I followed him down, hitting him on the port quarter with a long burst of fire. He was weaving, but flames were coming from his port wing. He disappeared into cloud and, following him, I came out dead on his tail at a range of about 100 yards. After another long burst, the aircraft went up in a sheet of flame.'

Heffer was credited with a Zero destroyed, and he was later awarded the DSC for his actions.

In the middle of August two new carriers headed for Sumatra to participate in Operation *Banquet*. *Victorious'* 47th NFW, under the command of Royal Marines ace Maj Ronnie Hay, shared fighter escort duties for the strikes with *Indomitable's* Hellcat-equipped 5th NFW (1839 and 1844 NASs), led by Lt Cdr T W Harrington. The latter was to claim three victories flying his personally marked aircraft in coming

Maj Ronnie Hay sits in the cockpit of his Corsair before the strikes on the Andaman and Nicobar Islands in October 1944 (*US National Archives via Jonathan Strickland*)

Corsair II JT383/7D of 1834 NAS aboard *Victorious* was the mount of Lt Leslie Durno during the strike on Car Nicobar on 19 October, when he shot down a Ki-43 and shared in the destruction of two others with Sub Lt Grave. Durno later became the Royal Navy's first Corsair ace (*US National Archives via Jonathan Strickland*)

weeks. Two of the squadrons involved in *Banquet* were also led by aces, namely Lt Cdr Noel Charlton of 1834 NAS and Lt Cdr Denis Jeram of 1839 NAS. The strike was made on 25 August, with the Corsairs concentrating on the airfield at Padang. Ronnie Hay recalled;

'After the attack, the fighters roamed the area looking for the most impressive buildings in the area. These would then be machine gunned in the hope that the Japanese overlords were in residence.'

To coincide with the American landings at Peleliu in mid September, *Victorious* and *Indomitable* undertook yet another diversionary attack when its aircraft struck the railway repair yard at Sigli, in Sumatra as part of Operation *Light B*. However, poor weather, compounded by the inexperience of the Royal Navy aircrews, meant that the results from the mission were disappointing. An intensive training programme was duly instituted upon the vessels' return to Ceylon.

One month later the carriers sallied on Operation *Millet*, which saw further diversionary raids made on the Nicobar Islands to coincide with US landings in the Philippines. Attacks began on 17 October and continued until the 19th, during which time Royal Navy Hellcats made their first claims against Japanese aircraft.

At 0840 hrs on the 19th the force was located by the enemy. An hour later the fleet's fighters engaged a raid by 12 'Oscars' of the 1st Reserve Flying Unit. In a fierce 40 minute fight, the enemy was driven off, but at the cost of two Corsairs and a Hellcat shot down. Sub Lt Leslie Durno of *Victorious'* 1834 NAS destroyed one of the Ki-43s and shared two more, whilst 1836 NAS's Lt Edmundson also downed an 'Oscar'.

Hellcat pilots from *Indomitable* found the enemy's top cover of three more Ki-43s, and in a short, sharp fight, they were shot down – two fell to Sub Lt Edward Wilson of the SANF, serving with 1844 NAS. After this action, Maj Ronnie Hay commented;

'The Corsair was just the right aircraft for that war. It was certainly better than anything we had, and an improvement of the Hellcat. It was more robust and faster, and although the Japanese could out-turn us in combat, we could out-climb, out-dive and out-gun him. By far the most healthy improvement was its endurance, as with about five hours worth of fuel in your tanks you didn't have the agony of wondering whether or not you would make it back to the carrier.'

THE SUMATRAN OILFIELDS

To support US operations in the Pacific, and an eventual invasion of Japan, a significant British fleet was proposed. Accordingly in Ceylon on 22 November 1944, Adm Sir Bruce Fraser hoisted his flag as C-in-C of the newly formed British Pacific Fleet (BPF), which was formed around the Eastern Fleet's three armoured fleet carriers. They were later joined by sister ships *Formidable, Indefatigable* and *Implacable*.

The following month, as part of Operation *Outflank*, the BPF began a series of strikes against the oil production and storage facilities in Sumatra that were so critical to the Japanese. However, because of bad weather, the port of Belawan Deli was attacked instead.

However, the BPF began the New Year successfully when, on 4 January 1945, *Indomitable, Victorious* and *Indefatigable* mounted Operation *Lentil* – a successful attack on the Pangkalan Brandan oil facilities. In spite of heavy flak and stiff opposition, the fighter pilots were credited with downing nine Ki-43s and destroying others on the ground at Medan and Tanjong Poera. During the attack, the Firefly achieved its first air combat success when Lt Levitt of 1770 NAS downed a Ki-43, while Sub Lt Phil Stott shared another with Sub Lt Redding. The fighter sweeps over Medan, and other airfields, were described as 'a field day'.

As he roared over Medan, Lt Leslie Durno of 1834 NAS spotted a Ki-46 'Dinah' in the circuit with its wheels and flaps down. Followed by his No 2, Sub Lt J H Richards, they climbed, and Richards opened fire. Damaged in this first pass, the Ki-46 was then targeted by Leslie Durno, who positioned himself behind the aircraft and fired a five-second burst

Corsair II JT427 was the personally coded aircraft of Maj Ronnie Hay, who was the Wing Leader of 47 NFW aboard *Victorious* in October 1944. He flew this aircraft during the Sumatran oil refinery strikes of January 1945, when he claimed two and two shared victories (*US National Archives via Jonathan Strickland*)

into the hapless enemy from just 50 yards. The 'Dinah' staggered slightly and then blew up, with the wreckage falling onto the edge of the airfield. Durno was so close that he too was almost brought down when his Corsair flew through the fireball and was hit by pieces of wreckage. The rugged fighter emerged from the flames unscathed, however.

Suitably encouraged by this initial success, Durno spotted a Ki-21 'Sally' bomber a few minutes later. Closing on it, he opened fire with an eight-second burst from 200 yards and observed strikes all over the engine and fuselage that set the aircraft on fire. Durno then saw the bomber's fin break off, followed seconds later by its port wing. In its death throes, Durno reported that he could see the two pilots in the cockpit fighting to get out, although neither did. He had thus become the first Royal Navy Corsair ace, and the first to claim five victories against the Japanese.

The main strike took off about 90 minutes after the fighter 'Ramrods', and among the close escort to the Avenger strike was Sub Lt D J Sheppard of 1836 NAS who, at 0850 hrs, spotted an 'Oscar' just below him. As he closed, the enemy fighter dived away, then pulled up in a desperate attempt to out turn the Corsair. Don Sheppard later recalled;

'The Jap's cockpit seemed to glow as I hit him with a long burst, and I could see the bullets striking the engine and cockpit. He levelled out at 300 ft and then went into a climbing right hand turn. I fired again and the pilot baled out as the aircraft rolled over and went into the sea. I watched the pilot land in the water, but he appeared to be dead.'

Ten minutes after claiming his first victory, the 24 year-old Sheppard spotted another Ki-43 and, once again, closed in before opening fire. The lightly built 'Oscar' blew up under this devastating burst and crashed into the sea. Sheppard then headed back to *Victorious*.

However, many of the close escorts forgot their charges and went after the Japanese fighters, but as 1836 NAS's Lt J B Edmundson said with some feeling, 'It's not every month of the year that you see a "Zero" in the Fleet Air Arm, so you can hardly blame a fighter pilot for making the most of his opportunities!'

The first major operation for the British Pacific Fleet carriers was the highly successful series of strikes that targeted the Japanese-held oil refineries in Sumatra. Seen unfolding its wings aboard *Indefatigable* for the first strike on 4 January 1945 is Firefly I DV126/4-C of 1770 NAS (*P H T Green Collection*)

Leslie Durno of 1834 NAS is one of the Royal Navy's least known aces, having achieved this status on 4 January 1945. During the final oil strike on the 29th of that month, his Corsair was hit by flak over Palembang and he was forced to bale out. Tragically, no trace of the young Canadian was ever found (*US National Archives via Jonathan Strickland*)

The Corsair squadrons in *Victorious* drew the following rare compliment from no less a person than the Director of Naval Air Warfare following *Lentil*. 'These two units have rendered most satisfactory combat reports, displaying good tactics and good shooting.'

Other pilots had also been successful, including Sub Lt Bill Foster (flying his wing leader's aircraft) of 1844 NAS, who shared in the destruction of a Ki-43 over the target. 1839 NAS's Sub Lt Richard Neal also got an 'Oscar';

'Whizzing about over Pangkalan Brandan, I felt a creepy feeling underneath and rolled over. Beneath me was an "Oscar" on the same course. I could see the pilot's hands, knees and feet. I immediately rolled and climbed madly without him seeing me. The rest was a no contest, as his aircraft caught fire immediately I attacked. The "Oscar" was fragile, and certainly not well flown – I felt guilty.'

Seated second from right in this group shot of 1836 NAS pilots is 21-year-old Canadian Sub Lt Don Sheppard, who also 'made ace' during the Palembang raids (*D J Sheppard*)

Seeing their first action in the Far East during this operation were the Seafires of the 24th NFW embarked in *Indefatigable*, but their limited range restricted them to fleet defence.

The major focus of the *Outflank* series of attacks, however, was the complex of refineries around Palembang, on the banks of the Moesi River on the north-east coast of Sumatra. The attacking force had to fly more than 150 miles into enemy held territory to reach the target, but an effective strike would deal a severe blow to the Japanese war effort.

The BPF's four carriers – *Illustrious, Indomitable, Victorious* and *Indefatigable* – had Pladjoe as the first target of Operation *Meridian 1*, which was launched on 24 January. In addition to providing an escort for the Avenger bombers, as well as flying combat air patrols (CAPs) in defence of the fleet, the fighters would also conduct 'Ramrods' over enemy airfields and perform flak suppression.

The first strike had four groups of escorts, plus Maj Ronnie Hay performing the air coordinator's role with his flight. Top cover comprised 11 Corsairs from *Victorious*, with strike close escort flown by 12 Fireflies, stern escort by eight Corsairs from 1833 NAS (led by Lt Cdr Hanson) and middle cover coming from eight Corsairs from 1830 NAS. Elsewhere, four Hellcats escorted a strike on the airfield at Mana, while 24 Corsairs from *Victorious* and *Illustrious* flew airfield sweeps.

As they swept in, Ki-44 'Tojos' from the 87th Sentai were led off by 1Lt Hideaki Inayama. A fierce dogfight ensued, with Ronnie Hay claiming one of the first successes over Tardjoengradi when, about ten minutes into the action, he spotted a 'Tojo' approaching from out of the sun;

'It was 0825 hrs, and after a five-minute chase I caught him at nought feet at 250 knots. Then I gave him a stern shot of two seconds, which hit his tail and engine and he crashed and broke up, but did not burn.'

Hay then climbed back to monitor the attack, and after two photographic runs over the steaming Sumatran jungle, he shot down another fighter. Also increasing their scores were Sub Lt Don Sheppard of 1836 NAS, who was credited with a 'Tojo', while in Firefly pilot Sub Lt Phil Stott of 1770 NAS shared in the destruction of two 'Oscars' from the 26th Sentai. And it was during this action that Sub Lt Edward Taylor became the only South African Navy ace when he shot down a 'Tojo' at around 0800 hrs. Fifteen minutes later, he also shared in the destruction of a twin-engined Ki-45 'Nick' from Maj Sato's 21st Sentai.

Maj Hay later wrote about the attack in the *London Gazette*;

'Throughout the attack the enemy had just sufficient fighters to saturate the escort. Fights were raging all over the target area. The presence of so many fighters showed that the "Ramrods" had not managed to keep the enemy's head down. Flown off in the second range, they were just too late over the airstrips to prevent "Zekes", "Tojos" and "Oscars" from taking off.'

In spite of his concerns about the escort, Hay concluded that 'this has been one of the better strikes the Fleet Air Arm has ever accomplished'.

After refuelling and replenishment, the fleet returned to strike at the other oil complex at Soengei Gerong on 29 January 1945. A heavy belt of rain and cloud delayed the launch, and the inbound strike encountered further bad weather. Hay again acted as the air coordinator, with Lt Cdr C C Tomkinson leading the close escort, Lt Cdr T W Harrington the mid cover of 16 Hellcats and Lt Percy Cole the top cover Corsairs. Once more the fighters provided CAP, escort and flew 'Ramrods'. With Japanese fighter opposition again in evidence, there were many combats. Over the target after the bombing was finished, Hay was attacked, as he recalled;

'I soon had to change my mind as a "Tojo" was coming for us. In shooting this one down, we descended to nought feet and, attracted by the gunfire, an "Oscar" came along. By 0905 hrs he too was dead.'

No 1836 NAS's Don Sheppard also claimed his fifth success;

Heading over the side of *Indomitable* on 27 February 1945 is Hellcat II JX758/5A of 1839 NAS. Prior to its watery demise, this aircraft had been assigned to unit CO Lt Cdr Shotten, who had made two claims in it on 24 January. Five days later, during the Soengei Gerong refinery attacks, New Zealander Lt Richard Mackie shot down a Ki-43 for the second of his three victories (*via H Holmes*)

'This inquisitive fellow was an "Oscar", and obviously attracted by the smoke of the earlier victim, he came to have a look. Hay ordered his flight of three aircraft to climb and not engage. This we did until we had a 1500-ft height advantage, when the leader and I then attacked. It was a vigorous dogfight and, after a series of steep turns, the Jap settled down for a moment, straight and level. My shells hit the pilot's cockpit, which glowed with a dull red as the bullets slammed home, then he rolled over and crashed into the trees.'

This Ki-43 was just one of 30 Japanese aircraft shot down that day.

As the strike recovered, Sub Lt Kernaghan of 887 NAS on a Seafire CAP shot down a 'Dinah' spotted approaching the Fleet. A short while later, New Zealander Sub Lt Keith McLennan of 1844 NAS, who was manning the alert Hellcat on *Indomitable*'s flightdeck, was launched as seven Ki-21 'Sally' and Ki-48 'Lily' bombers of the 'Shichisi Mitate' Special Attack Corps, led by Maj Hitoyuki Kato, approached on suicide attacks at low level. One of his squadron colleagues later wrote, 'He took off and shot two of them down "just like that". I saw his camera gun film'. McLennan also shared in the destruction of a third with a Seafire of 894 NAS flown by Sub Lt Elson. Having taken his total to $3^1/2$ destroyed, he had become the most successful Royal New Zealand Navy pilot of the war.

After this series of attacks, the BPF continued on to its operational base in Australia, arriving in Sydney in mid-February in preparation for operations in the Pacific.

OKINAWA

In early March 1945 the fleet moved to its forward base at Manus, in the Admiralty Islands, ready to play its part in the invasion of Okinawa – code

On 24 January 1945, Corsair II JT443 (bottom right) was used by Lt Percy Cole of 1833 NAS to shoot down a Ki-45 'Nick' for his second victory. The aircraft is seen here on the bow of *Illustrious* soon after returning from the mission. Note the Barracudas parked amongst the Corsairs (*Admiralty via R S G Mackay*)

name Operation *Iceberg*. Sailing as Task Force (TF) 57 within the US Fifth Fleet, the BPF, with its four carriers, was given the job of neutralising airfields in the Sakishima Gunto archipelago to prevent air reinforcement of Okinawa from Formosa. Commencing on 26 March, it was to be a necessary, if thankless, task. The Hellcats and Corsairs flew escort missions while *Indefatigable's* Seafires performed fleet CAP. A routine of two strike days followed by replenishment soon ensued.

The US landings on Okinawa began on 1 April, and the fanatical Japanese response included launching waves of *kamikaze* aircraft – over the next month, all the British carriers were hit.

That day, the first fighter 'Ramrods' had been launched when, just after 0700 hrs, an inbound raid was detected, probably of *kamikazes*. The 'Ramrods' were quickly recalled and the CAP waded into the enemy. Just before 0730 hrs a Zero machine gunned the battleship HMS *King George V* then, as it dived towards *Indefatigable*, was pounced on by Sub Lt Richard Reynolds in an 894 NAS Seafire. The fighter evaded all attempts to engage it, but Reynolds' fire continued to hit home, his Seafire only breaking off just before the enemy struck the carrier. In spite of the damage inflicted by the first *kamikaze* to hit a British carrier, *Indefatigable* was receiving aircraft 40 minutes later.

Some 20 minutes after this first attack, Richard Reynolds attacked a second Zero that had just dive-bombed the anti-aircraft cruiser HMS *Ulster Queen*. Having swiftly sent the fighter down with two short bursts, he then latched onto a third Zero, which turned into the Seafire. His quarry was inviting Reynolds to commit to a turning fight, at which the Japanese fighter excelled. The experienced Seafire pilot maintained his speed, however, and in a series of 'yo-yo' attacks used his remaining ammunition to send his third victim of the morning to its destruction. In so doing, Reynolds became the Royal Navy's only Seafire ace.

Also successful that morning was 5th NFW leader Lt Cdr Tommy Harrington, who claimed his final victory;

'He was flying out of range and I carefully fired a good long blast over his port wing. He then very kindly obliged by executing a rather difficult turn to port, which enabled me to close and shoot this unhappy amateur down.'

Harrington's victim was an 'Oscar' thought to have also been flown by a *kamikaze* pilot.

It was not all good news for the fighter squadrons, however, as over the islands 1834 NAS lost its CO, Lt Cdr Hopkins, while the South

The only Seafire ace was Sub Lt Richard Reynolds of 894 NAS who, having shared in the destruction of two German flying-boats in the Arctic in August 1944, became an ace at the start of the Okinawa operation when he destroyed three *kamikazes*. His Seafire III (PR256), nicknamed *Merry Widow*, soon wore evidence of his success – a rare addition to a Royal Navy aircraft (*via C F Shores*)

African Edward Wilson had his engine hit over Ishigaki and he was forced to ditch. He was lucky enough to be picked up by the Air-Sea Rescue Walrus from *Victorious*.

A few days later another Hellcat pilot from 1844 NAS opened his account when, during his first raid on Miyako airfield, Sub Lt Bill Atkinson from Manitoba attacked a G4M 'Betty' bomber, but could only claim it as probably destroyed. However, at about 1730 hrs on 6 April he went one better by sharing

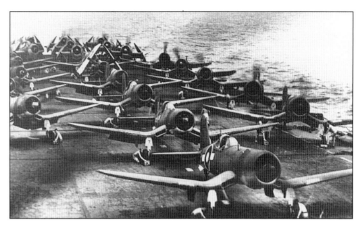

in the destruction of a D4M 'Judy' dive-bomber with Lt Edward Wilson south of Nansei Shoto. This kill duly took Wilson's tally to seven aircraft destroyed, thus making him the Royal Navy's leading Hellcat ace.

On 12 April TF 57 moved at American request to hit targets in Formosa, with *Victorious*' Lt Col Ronnie Hay once again acting as air coordinator during the strike on Matsuyama airfield. That morning a pair of Fireflies from *Indefatigable*'s 1770 NAS, flown by Lt Bill Thomson and Sub Lt Phil Stott, were escorting a US Navy PBM Mariner flying-boat on an air-sea rescue mission when they spotted five Ki-51 'Sonia' bombers. Breaking off, the Firefly pilots each shot down two (the fifth 'Sonia' was probably destroyed), and in the process Stott became the Royal Navy's only Firefly ace. Thomson recorded in his log book;

'CAP over rescue Mariner (US). Sighted five "Sonias" 12 miles northwest of south-west point Kumi Island at 1000 ft. Climbed and attacked from 2000 ft port quarter. Shot down port stern aircraft in flames, then chased his wingman, who evaded me for a while – finally closed, and at

During the Okinawa operations, *Victorious*' 47th NFW continued to be led by Lt Col Ronnie Hay – seen here sat in his Corsair II (JT456) at the head of a strike in May 1945 (*R C Hay*)

The only Firefly ace was Sub Lt Phil Stott (second from right) of *Indefatigable*'s 1770 NAS who, on 12 April 1945, shot down two of the four Ki-51 'Sonias' destroyed off Formosa. To Stott's right is his observer Lt Ward, whilst the other crewmen are Sub Lt Miller (extreme right) and Lt Bill Thomson (extreme left), who also shot down two Ki-51s (*B Thomson*)

50 yards he exploded in red flames. Resumed patrol. No 2 got two more. I claim two "Sonias" certain.'

The Hellcat had also enjoyed its most successful day in British service, as no less than six enemy fighters had been shot down by the type. Two of these fell to Sub Lt Bill Foster who, at 0630 hrs, had destroyed a Ki-43 and a Ki-61 'Tony'. His colleague Bill Atkinson also claimed a Ki-61 probably destroyed, as well as a Zero destroyed.

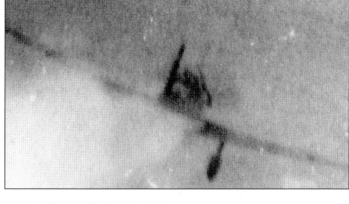

The demise of one of the four Ki-51s downed by 1770 NAS Fireflies on 12 April 1945 was caught on film by the camera gun fitted to Lt Bill Thomson's aircraft (*B Thomson*)

The Seafire CAP was also engaged when 887 NAS's Sub Lt J H Kernaghan attacked a mixed formation of enemy fighters which broke and evaded. Chasing after them, Kernaghan fired two long bursts at a Zero as it dived away, causing it to catch fire and crash into the sea. As it fell, Kernaghan was already turning after a Ki-61, which he damaged with his remaining ammunition.

The fleet returned to the Sakishima Gunto to resume operations on the 14th, and saw further action the next day when, amongst other claims, a flight of Hellcats, that included Bill Atkinson, shot down a C6M 'Myrt'.

HMS *Formidable* had replaced *Illustrious*, but the newcomer had a savage initiation, for on its first day of operating (the 16th) 1842 NAS lost its CO, Lt Cdr 'Judy' Garland, when his Corsair was shot down over Ishigaki. That day Bill Foster shot down a 'Myrt', and when he repeated this feat five days later he achieved coveted ace status. Soon afterwards the fleet retired to Leyte to replenish and refit.

After a brief rest, the BPF returned to hit the Sakishima airfields once more, bombing Miyako on 4 May. However, with the BPF's heavy ships detached to bombard the coast, the enemy threw in further suicide attacks on the carriers. On CAP were Sub Lts Richard Reynolds and Randall Kay, who both again successfully used 'yo-yo' attacks to bring down a 'Hamp'. This would be Reynolds final success, although Kay was to make further claims in the final combat of the war. Although *Indomitable's* Hellcats also played their part that day by claiming three intruders, they could not stop their carrier, or *Formidable*, being struck by *kamikazes*.

One of the pilots who became an ace during operations off the Sakishima Gunto was Sub Lt Bill Foster, who flew Hellcats from *Indomitable* with 1844 NAS (*R S G Mackay*)

Attacks on the apparently empty airfields continued, but so did the *kamikaze* attacks. At around 1700 hrs on 9 May, in good weather, both *Formidable* and *Victorious* were hit, losing 47 Corsairs between them. Once again, however, both vessels were soon operational. These attacks proved to be the last of their kind aimed at the BPF, and on 25 May, with Okinawa largely in American hands, the fleet flew its final strikes. The BPF then retired south to refit its battered ships and replenish its aircraft, having spent 62 days at sea during the Okinawa operations. Its fighters had claimed 42 Japanese aircraft shot down and many more destroyed on the ground. The fleet arrived back in Sydney in early June.

THE LAND OF THE RISING SUN

The fleet was joined by the new carrier HMS *Implacable* following the refit period. The vessel's fighter complement included the Seafires of 801

and 880 NASs, with the latter unit led by Lt Cdr Mike Crosley. The ship's Commander (Air), Cdr Charles Evans, was also an ace.

By way of an introduction to the Pacific, on 14 June 1945 HMS *Implacable's* Air Group mounted a raid on the now-bypassed and neutralised Japanese base at Truk, in the Caroline Islands. The carrier

arrived at the fleet's forward base at Manus on the 17th to join *Formidable*, *Victorious* and *Indefatigable*. As *Indomitable* was undergoing a refit at the time, six of its Hellcats from 1844 NAS transferred to *Formidable* for nightfighting duties.

The US fleet had begun hitting targets around Tokyo in mid July, and it was joined by the Royal Navy on the 17th, when a 'Ramrod' of Corsairs from *Formidable* and Fireflies from *Implacable's* 1771 NAS attacked airfields at Sendai, Masuda and Matsushima, about 250 miles north of Tokyo. They thus became the first British aircraft to fly over the Japanese home islands. Later in the day, another 'Ramrod', led by 1834 NAS's CO, Lt Cdr J G Baldwin, took off from *Victorious* and flew across Honshu to hit targets on the Japanese west coast.

Also flying their first 'Ramrods' were *Implacable's* Seafires, which also provided CAP against expected attacks by Japanese *kamikazes* – the Seafires carried old Kittyhawk drop tanks, which significantly extended their range. The weather, however, prevented any action against the enemy. The following day, Lt Cdr Crosley led an attack on airfields on the Japanese mainland and shipping in the Inland Sea. Much light flak was encountered and losses soon began to mount, particularly within the Corsair squadrons.

The BPF, now designated Task Force 37, withdrew for replenishment before returning for a further series of strikes against airfields and installations. 880 NAS CO Lt Cdr Mike Crosley led one 'Ramrod' and

On moving into the Pacific, the aircraft of the BPF adopted barred US-style national markings, as shown in this excellent view of Corsair II JT633/P120 of 1834 NAS, flown by Lt Wally Knight from HMS *Victorious*. Sub Lt Pocock used this aircraft to share in the destruction of a 'Myrt' reconnaissance aircraft over the Sakishima Gunto on 4 May 1945 (*G J Thomas*)

During the Okinawa operation, all of the BPF carriers were struck at least once by *kamikazes*. However, thanks to their armoured flightdecks they generally suffered only superficial damage, as was the case with *Formidable*, which was hit on 4 May 1945. This photograph of the battle-scarred carrier was taken soon after it had been struck (*D N Davis*)

The newest of the carriers assigned to the BPF was HMS *Implacable*, which arrived in the Pacific after the Okinawa operation. Its air wing saw extensive combat over Japan in the final weeks of the war (*P H T Green Collection*)

Implacable's Firefly squadron was 1771 NAS, led by Lt Cdr MacWhirter. He is seen here flying his personal aircraft (DK431/N275 *Evelyn Tensions*), armed with rocket projectiles, on his way to attack targets in Japan in July 1945 (*R MacWhirter*)

attacked the seaplane bases at Tokushima, on the northern entrance to the Inland Sea, and Konatsushima, as he later described;

'Our target was easy to find on the coast. It was also in a clear patch of weather. I aimed at a twin-engined aircraft – none of us stayed long enough to find out how we had got on. On the way back, we dived at Konatsushima. Here, the flak was very easy to see. They had obviously had warning from our attack further up the coast, so the gunners were ready for us. There were several twin-floated aeroplanes drawn up on the sloping concrete slipways, and we hit many of them. It was rewarding to see our cannon shells exploding in bright flashes in the dawn light as they hit the slipways around the targets. Once again the attack was all over in ten seconds or so, and none of us were hit by flak.'

Crosley had damaged a large four-engine H6K 'Mavis' flying-boat at Tokushima, whilst at Konatsushima he had destroyed an F1M 'Pete'. Sadly, one Seafire was lost during the return flight. Later that afternoon, Crosley led another 'Ramrod';

'Our target was Takamatsu airfield, supposedly crammed with 50 aircraft. Our briefing showed that it also had 120 guns surrounding it, and we were told to expect fighters too. The weather was much better than we had expected, and we were able to employ our usual attack system. We hardly saw any flak. I aimed at a "Myrt".'

The following evening (25 July), as the fleet was withdrawing to refuel, a small group of 'bogeys' appeared on radar. The four 'dusk' patrol Hellcats from the 1844 NAS detachment embarked in *Formidable* were airborne at the time, and they were quickly vectored onto a quartet of Aichi B7A 'Grace' torpedo-bombers flying at 20,000 ft on a heading for the ships. The Hellcats, flown by Sub Lts Atkinson, Foster, Mackie and

The Fleet Air Arm also conducted missions off Burma in 1945, with these Seafires from 807 NAS (embarked in HMS *Hunter*) seeing sporadic action. During the cruise NN300/D5O was stripped of paint and assigned to wing leader, Lt Cdr George Baldwin. It was being flown by Sub Lt Gardner on 16 May 1945, however, when it damaged a Ki-43 over Sumatra (*G J Thomas*)

Flying from *Implacable*, 880 NAS's Seafires ranged over Japan during the last weeks of the war. The unit was only able to perform these missions thanks to the ship's unofficial acquisition of some old P-40 drop tanks, which dramatically increased the Seafire's notoriously short endurance (*P R Arnold Collection*)

Sub Lt Speak puts Hellcat II JZ935/W145 of 1844 NAS into the barrier after a strike. Note that the barrier cabling has bitten deep into the fighter's cowling (*via R C Sturtivant*)

Taylor, made short work of the rarely seen B7As, as is described in the official Royal Canadian Navy history;

'During his attachment to *Formidable*, Atkinson achieved a rare distinction on the night of 25 July. Four Hellcats were scrambled on a night combat air patrol. These were conventional Hellcat IIs without radar, but their pilots had been trained in night flying. Shortly after assuming patrol, incoming Japanese aircraft were detected. Two Hellcats were forced to return to the carrier unserviceable. Sub Lt Atkinson assumed the lead of the remaining two Hellcats and was vectored out on an intercepting course.

'Under a full moon, Atkinson identified the bandits as big, single-engined "Grace" torpedo-bombers, and took his New Zealand wingman, Sub Lt R F Mackie, into the attack. Atkinson latched onto a pair of "Graces" and shot them both into the water, while Mackie dumped the third. Then, in routing the other bandits, a fourth "Grace" went down and the enemy attack was completely broken up.

'A tragedy was also averted following the action that same night. Mackie lost his electrical system and radios in the skirmish and became disoriented. Having lost Atkinson, he had no means of locating the distant blacked-out carrier. Fortunately, as Atkinson came in to land and

The last Commonwealth pilot to become an ace was Canadian Lt Bill Atkinson (right). He achieved the coveted status on 25 July 1945 whilst flying Hellcats with the 1844 NAS detachment embarked in *Formidable*. His wingman on this occasion was New Zealander Sub Lt Richard Mackie (left), who claimed his third victory during the same engagement (*Canadian Forces*)

Corsair IV KD658/X115 of 1841 NAS sits lashed to the deck of HMS *Formidable* off the Japanese coast in July 1945. The aircraft was lost in action on 9 August when Canadian Lt R H 'Hammy' Gray pressed home his attack on a Japanese destroyer in Onagawa Bay. He was subsequently awarded a posthumous Victoria Cross for his actions (*Canadian Forces*)

the carrier was illuminated, Mackie saw the distant flash of light and flew safely back to *Formidable*.'

These successes made Bill Atkinson the last Commonwealth pilot to become an ace during World War 2.

Strikes by TF 37 aircraft against airfield and shipping targets continued, with 264 offensive and 135 defensive sorties being flown on 27 July alone. The following day there were further strikes against Inland Sea targets, and the naval base at Maisuru, on the northern coast of Honshu, was attacked by Corsairs of *Formidable's* 1841 NAS. Four ships were sunk or damaged and several aircraft downed. For his leadership and determination during these attacks, the unit's senior pilot, Lt 'Hammy' Gray, was awarded a DSC.

Although operations continued, they were hampered by the bad weather that marked the onset of the typhoon season, and combined with the pause before the attack on Hiroshima, the next series of operations did not begin until 9 August. One of the first 'Ramrods' flown on this date comprised eight Corsairs from *Formidable* led by Lt 'Hammy' Gray. The following account is from the Royal Canadian Navy's official history;

'At Onagawa Bay, the fliers found below a number of Japanese ships and dived in to attack. Furious fire was opened on the aircraft from army batteries on the ground and from warships in the Bay. Lt Gray selected for his target an enemy destroyer. He swept in oblivious of the concentrated fire and made straight for his target. His aircraft was hit and hit again, but he kept on. As he came close to the destroyer, Lt Gray's aeroplane caught fire, but he pressed on to within 50 ft of the Japanese ship before releasing his bombs. He scored at least one direct hit, possibly more. The destroyer sank almost immediately. Lt Gray did not return. He had given his life at the very end of his fearless bombing run.'

For Lt Gray's great gallantry and self-sacrifice, on 13 November the award of a posthumous Victoria Cross to him was announced. He became only the second fighter pilot to receive a VC in World War 2.

On 9 and 10 August aircraft from the British carriers flew more than 500 offensive sorties in a series of air strikes on airfields and shipping in northern Honshu. The last planned strike day on the 12th was cancelled due to weather, after which most of the BPF left the area due to a lack of fuel. Only *Indefatigable* remained, its units continuing operations. For most, however, the war was over.

FULL CIRCLE

With the Japanese on the point of surrender, *Indefatigable*'s Avengers from 820 NAS, along with the Fireflies of 1772 NAS and the Seafires of 887 and 894 NASs, continued their attacks on the enemy mainland. On 13 August 1945, air attacks concentrated in the Tokyo area once more, and soon after dawn on the 15th, eight Seafires (led by Sub Lt Hockley) left *Indefatigable*'s deck to escort an Avenger strike on Kisarazu airfield. However, due to the weather, they switched to an alternative target in Odaki Bay.

At about 0545 hrs, as the formation crossed the bay, two Zeros were seen, although it was suspected that they might be decoys. This proved to be the case, as a dozen more were then seen diving on the British formation from behind. Unfortunately, possibly due to R/T failure, Freddie Hockley, who was in the lead, did not react and was shot down on the Zeros' first pass. He managed to bale out, however, but was quickly captured and, in a dreadful act of vengeful savagery, was then beheaded – the last Royal Navy casualty of the war. However, the remainder of the Seafires then waded into the Japanese fighters.

Sub Lt Vic Lowden of 887 NAS deployed his flight in line abreast at the second Japanese element, as the first was out of range. He opened fire with his cannon at the second Zero from the right from a range of about 800 yards and recorded that the undercarriage oleos dropped, and that it 'flamed nicely, going down'. His No 3, Sub Lt 'Taffy' Williams, had also hit this aircraft, so the victory was shared. Lowden then switched his fire to the aircraft on the extreme right, and with slight deflection from about 200 yards, saw pieces fly off as this too fell away. He wrote afterwards;

'I then found one of the original attacking "Zekes" climbing at 8000 ft about 1000 yards from me. I closed to 100 yards at 11,000 ft, kicking on the rudder to have a look at the markings, and then went back astern and fired two two-second bursts of machine gun fire – the cannon ammunition had already been exhausted. Following strikes all over the aircraft, the pilot baled out. His fighter dived past him, smoking somewhat.'

Lowden had hit five of the enemy, being credited with two destroyed, a third shared and the other two damaged. Aside from the shared kill, 'Taffy' Williams shot down a second Zero as well. 887 NAS's Sub Lt 'Spud' Murphy, flying NN212/S112, also shot down two enemy fighters. He later recalled;

'The enemy approached our Avengers in fairly close starboard echelon, but with flights in line

Seafire III NN212/S112 of 887 NAS, seen here in an unfortunate pose, was flown by Sub Lt 'Spud' Murphy during the final air engagement of the war. He shot down two A6M Zeros in a brief dogfight over Odaki Bay on 15 August 1945. The Japanese surrender was announced soon afterwards (*C Earle*)

astern. They peeled off smartly in fours from down sun and headed for the Avengers. One section of four appeared to be coming head-on for us, but I didn't observe their guns firing. Their original attack was well coordinated, but they seemed to lose each other after that, and could not have kept a good lookout astern.

'Opened fire with my flight leader from the enemy's port quarter. Saw strikes on fuselage of enemy, which was finished off by flight leader or No 3. Disengaged from above to attack another "Zeke" to port and 500 ft below. Closed from above and astern, obtaining hits on belly and engine. His undercart fell down and smoke and flame were coming from engine, but I was closing too fast and overshot. Pulled up nose to re-attack No 2 and saw lone 'Zeke' at same level doing a shallow turn to starboard. He evidently didn't see me, and I held fire till some 100 yards away. Observed immediate strikes on cockpit and engine, which burst into flames. Enemy rolled on back, plummeting in flames into cloud.'

Murphy also noted that the accuracy of the Japanese fire was poor, with not enough deflection, and that due to an early sighting by the formation leader, the Seafires had managed to get into a good tactical position.

From the Avengers' close escort, Sub Lt Don Duncan of 894 NAS kept his manoeuvring speed up and engaged three of the Zeros, one of which he probably destroyed before he suffered a jammed cannon. His section leader, Sub Lt Randy Kay, made a quarter attack on another of the A6Ms as it attacked his charges and set it on fire in the port wing root, before switching fire to another fighter with a high deflection shot as it crossed his nose. Kay's first burst was devastating, blowing the tail off this aircraft. He then hit a third Zero.

The Seafire's previous air combats in the Pacific had been on 9 May 1945 off Okinawa during the final day of *kamikaze* attacks on the BPF, so this was an outstanding and successful end to its career. Indeed, the 24th NFW pilots were credited with seven fighters destroyed, three probables and four damaged, with an eighth Zero felled by an Avenger gunner. Soon after they had returned to *Indefatigable*, the Seafire pilots learned that operations were to be cancelled at 0700 hrs the following morning, with a ceasefire brought into effect shortly thereafter.

When it had claimed the first confirmed British aerial victory of World War 2 in September 1939, the Royal Navy's aircraft carriers embarked only a few fighters with very limited capabilities. Appropriately, almost six years later, Fleet Air Arm fighters also made the final British claims of the conflict, but by then the Royal Navy had a fleet of armoured carriers operating on the other side of the world. Able to remain at sea for long periods, these ships were operating hundreds of world class fighters.

No less than 36 naval pilots had become aces during the war, and a further 18 had made a total of five claims or more.

The Fleet Air Arm had come full circle.

The successful pilots of the 24th NFW's last wartime engagement. They are, from left to right, Sub Lts Don Duncan (894 NAS – 2 probables), Randy Kay (894 NAS – 1 destroyed, 1 probable and 1 damaged), 'Spud' Murphy (887 NAS – 2 destroyed), Vic Lowden (887 NAS – 2 and 1 shared destroyed and 2 damaged), Ted Garvin (894 NAS – 1 damaged) and 'Taffy' Williams (887 NAS – 1 and 1 shared destroyed) (*Author's Collection*)

APPENDICES

APPENDIX 1

Royal Navy Aces

Name	Service	NAS/Sqn	Total	Remarks
Orr S G	RNVR	806, 896, 804	6+8sh/0.5/-	
Sewell A J	RNVR	806, 804, 1837	6+7sh/0.5/3+2sh	
Hay R C	RM	801, 808, 809, No 47 NFW	4+9sh/0.5/3sh	Royal Marines' only ace
Hogg G A	RNVR	806	4+8sh/-/-	
Cork R J	RN	242, 880, 15th NFW	9+2sh/1/4	
Gardner R E	RNVR	242, 807, 889	6+4sh/1/-	
Evans C L G	RN	803, 806	2+8sh/0.5/-	
Dawson-Paul F	RN	64	7.5/-/1	
Barnes W L L	RN	806	6+2sh/-/6+2sh	
Bruen J M	RN	802, 801, 803, 800	5+3sh/-/2.5	
Tillard R C	RN	808	6.5/-/-	
Atkinson W H I	RCNVR	1844	5+2sh/2/-(?)	Royal Canadian Navy top scorer?
Ritchie B	RNVR	800	5+2sh/-/-	
Wilson E T	SANF(V)	1844	3+4sh/-/-	Only South African Naval Force ace
Macdonald-Hall R	RN	806, 807	1+6sh/1/2	
Taylour E W T	RN	800, 808, 802	1+6sh/1/?	
Hallett N N	RN	807, 884, 887	7sh/0.5/4sh	24th and 3rd NFWs
Brabner R A	RNVR	806, 805, 801	5.5/1/1	
Jeram D M	RN	213, 888, 1839	5.5/1/-	
Sheppard D J	RCNVR	1835, 1836	4+2sh/1/-	
Sparke P D J	RN	806	4+2sh/-/-	
Charlton P N	RN	803, 800, 1834	3+3sh/2/1	
Reynolds R H	RNVR	894, 899	3+3sh/-/1	
Henley R S	RN	806	2+3sh/1/4	
Sabey A	RN	801, 802, 804, 800	2+3sh/-/1	
Lowe I L F	RN	806, 882, 898, 800	1+5sh/-/-	
Theobald A W	RN	803	1+4sh/-/1	
Lucy W P	RN	803	5sh/-/-	First Royal Navy Ace of World War 2
Crosley M R	RNVR	813 FF, 800, 804, 886, 880, 801	4.5/1/-	
Blake A G	RNVR	19	4.5/-/2	
Foster W M C	RNVR	1844	4.5/- /-	
Martyn W H	RN	801, 880	2+3sh/-/-	
Stott J P	RNVR	1770	2+3sh/-/-	
Durno L D	RNVR	1834	1+4sh/-/-	
Guthrie G C McE	RNVR	808	5sh/-/0.5	
Keighly-Peach C L*	RN	813 FF	3.5/1/- (possibly 4.5/-/-)	

APPENDIX 2

Non-Ace Pilots with Notable Claims

Name	Service	NAS/Sqn	Total	Remarks
Bird R A	RN	804, 881, 882	1+2sh/-/2	
Brokensha G W	RN	803, 888	3sh/-/2.5	
Duthie H E	RNZNVR	801	3sh/-/2	
Fell M F	RN	800, 806, 805, 878	3sh/1/-	
Gibson D C E F	RN	803	4sh/1/?	
Goodfellow A P	RNVR	808	3sh/-/2sh	
Gray R H	RCNVR	803, 877, 1841	-	Victoria Cross
Griffiths A S	RN	803, 806	2/-/3	
Hutton P J	RNVR	801, 805	3.5/2/0.5	
Keith L K	RN	813 FF, 805	1+2sh/-/2	
Lewin E D G	RN	880, 808, 885	4sh/-/2sh	
Lowden V S	RNVR	899, 887	2.5/-/2	
Massy P W V	RN	813, 806, 883	3/-/3	
McLennan K A	RNZNVR	1844	3.5/-/-	Top RNZN pilot
Moekardanoe H	RNethN	1839	1/-/-	Top RNethN pilot
Pennington F A J	RNZNVR	884, 889	4sh/?/?	
Price D R O	RNVR	29	3/-/2	Top nightfighter pilot
Smeeton R M	RN	804, 800	4sh/-/?	
Spurway K V V	RN	800	2.5/-/1?	
Taylor P E	RN	808	1.5/-/3sh	
Turnbull F R A	RN	801, 801, 894, 47th NFW	3sh/-/2	

APPENDIX 3

Leading Royal Navy Pilots by Type

Type	Name	Score	Total
Corsair	Sheppard D J	4+2sh/-/-	4+2sh/-/-
Firefly	Stott J P	2+3sh/-/-	2+3sh/-/-
Fulmar	Hogg G A	4+8sh/-/-	4+8sh/-/-
Hellcat	Wilson E T	3+4sh/-/-	3+4sh/-/-
Martlet/Wildcat	Cotching R A	2+2sh/-/-	2+2sh/-/-
Mosquito	Price D R O	3/-/2	3/-/2
Roc	Day A G	1/-/1	1/-/1
Sea Gladiator	Keighly-Peach C L	3.5/1/-	3.5/1/-
Sea Hurricane/Hurricane	Cork R J	9+2sh/1/4	9+2sh/1/4
Seafire	Reynolds R H	3+3sh/-/-	3+3sh/-/-
Skua	Lucy W P	7sh/1/3	7sh/1/3
Spitfire	Dawson-Paul F	7.5/-/-	7.5/-/-

Key

RN – Royal Navy
RNVR – Royal Navy Volunteer Reserve
RM – Royal Marines
RCNVR – Royal Canadian Navy Volunteer Reserve
SANF(V) – South African Naval Force(Volunteer)
RNZN – Royal New Zealand Navy
RNethN – Royal Netherlands Navy
NFW – Naval Fighter Wing
FF – Fighter Flight

Note – those pilots with less than five victories are marked thus * in Appendix 1, and are shown because of their inclusion in *Aces High* and where there may be doubt as to their actual scores

1

Roc I L3105 of 806 NAS, flown by Mid G A Hogg, Worthy Down, February 1940

Mid Graham Hogg joined 806 NAS soon after it had formed, the unit being at West Freugh, on the west coast of Scotland, conducting weapons training with its Skuas at the time of his arrival. The squadron's turret-equipped Rocs had been left at its base at Worthy Down, in Hampshire, and after returning there, Hogg also flew this ill-conceived type. Indeed, he flew this aircraft on a number of occasions during February and March 1940, when it wore the full unit codes for HMS *Illustrious*. During the Dunkirk evacuation, Hogg sortied both in the Skua and Roc, crash-landing at the end of his first operation after being attacked by 'friendly' fighters.

2

Skua II L2963 of 803 NAS, flown by Lt W P Lucy, HMS *Glorious*, Norway, 26 April 1940

The first Royal Navy pilot to become an ace during World War 2 was Lt Bill Lucy, who was also the CO of Skua-equipped 803 NAS. Making most of his claims flying from carriers off Norway, Lucy led a trio of Skuas in this aircraft from HMS *Glorious* (to which they were detached from *Ark Royal*) on a patrol on 26 April 1940. During the course of the mission he spotted three He 111s from I./KG 26 and attacked them immediately. One Skua was hit by return fire and force-landed, but Lucy and Lt Christian damaged a bomber. They then attacked He 111 L1+KT of 9./LG 1, which they forced down into Romsdalsfjord. This was Bill Lucy's second victory. His Skua had the undersides of its wings painted black (port) and white (starboard) for identification purposes.

3

Sea Gladiator N5517 of 813 NAS Fighter Flight, flown by Cdr C L Keighly-Peach, HMS *Eagle*, central Mediterranean, July 1940

HMS *Eagle*'s fighter flight, which formed in June 1940 with four Sea Gladiators, was led by the ship's Commander (Flying), Cdr Charles Keighly-Peach. Under him, the flight prospered over the succeeding weeks, destroying possibly as many as seven Italian bombers. 'K-P' claimed most of them, and he duly received a DSO for his successes. His first victory came on 11 July when he shot down an S.79, although he was slightly wounded in the leg. All five of Keighly-Peach's claims were made flying this aircraft, which, the following year, served in Crete with 805 NAS. N5517 was lost, along with its pilot, Lt P F Scott, when it force-landed in the sea some 100 miles south of the island on 15 May 1941.

4

Skua II L2927 of 803 NAS, flown by Lt J M Bruen, HMS *Ark Royal*, central Mediterranean, July-August 1940

One of the great Fleet Air Arm characters of the early war years was Lt 'Bill' Bruen, who had been flying fighters from carriers since 1936. When *Ark Royal* was operating in the Mediterranean during the summer of 1940, this Skua was his regular aircraft, and Bruen made all of his early claims whilst

flying L2927. The first were during the attack on the French fleet at Oran on 3 July, when he damaged two Vichy fighters and also shared in the destruction of a Breguet flying-boat. Then, on 31 August, Bruen was again at the Skua's controls when he destroyed two Italian shadowers.

5

Hurricane I V7203 of No 242 Sqn, flown by Sub Lt R E Gardner, Coltishall, July 1940

One of the Royal Navy pilots lent to the RAF in 1940, Sub Lt 'Jimmie' Gardner made his first claim on 10 July when he shot down an He 111 off Lowestoft. He became an ace in mid September, having taken part in the heavy fighting with No 242 Sqn in the intervening period. Although he made no claims in this aircraft, Gardner did fly it often from mid July, although it was actually the regular aircraft of Sgt Eric Richardson. RAF ace Flg Off John Latta was lost in V7203 during No 242 Sqn's first 'Circus' operation to France on 10 January 1941. Gardner went on to enjoy further successes whilst flying Fulmars from *Ark Royal* in the Mediterranean.

6

Fulmar I N1886 of 806 NAS, flown by Sub Lt I L F Lowe, HMS *Illustrious*, off Malta, 2 September 1940

806 NAS was the first squadron to take the Fulmar into action, and off Rhodes on 2 September 1940, Sub Lt Ivan Lowe was flying this aircraft with NA Kensett as his telegraphist air gunner in a section led by Lt Cdr Charles Evans. The Fulmars sighted a Cant Z.501, and diving in from astern, Lowe helped his CO and Lt Cdr Kilroy shoot down the Italian flying-boat to the cheers of the entire fleet. Lowe's first victory was also the Fulmar's first, and marked the start of his rise to 'acedom' – a status that he achieved two months later.

7

Sea Gladiator N5549 of 806 NAS, flown by Sub Lt A J Sewell, HMS *Illustrious*, central Mediterranean, 8 November 1940

This aircraft was one of two Sea Gladiators that were transferred to Fulmar-equipped 806 NAS to supplement the fighter defences of the recently arrived carrier HMS *Illustrious*. On 8 November 1940, N5549 was used by Sub Lt 'Jackie' Sewell to destroy an Italian Cant Z.501 flying-boat of 186ᵃ *Squadriglia* – this victory was shared with Sub Lt Roger Nichols in N5513. The Cant was Sewell's first claim with the Sea Gladiator, although he already had three and two shared victories to his credit in Fulmars from combat over the preceding two months. On 24 January 1941 he used a Sea Gladiator to shoot down a Ju 88 near Malta, this victory proving to be the biplane's final claim over the battered island.

8

Martlet III AX824 of 880 NAS, flown by Sub Lt R J Cork, Arbroath, 1 February 1941

880 NAS was the third unit to re-equip with the Martlet, operating three for just four weeks in early 1941, prior to a decision being made to equip the squadron with Sea

Hurricanes instead. One of the trio of aircraft issued to the unit was AX824 (nicknamed *Gertie*), which had non-folding wings and came from an ex-French contract. Battle of Britain ace Sub Lt Dickie Cork was one of 880 NAS's pilots at the time, and he flew Martlets until they were withdrawn on 16 February – he had flown AX824 from Arbroath for the first time on the 1st.

9
Buffalo I AS419 of 805 NAS, flown by Lt R A Brabner, Maleme, Crete, 19 March 1941
Three examples of the portly Buffalo were used by 805 NAS alongside its Fulmars for the air defence of the strategically important island of Crete. One of the unit's pilots at the time was Lt Rupert Brabner, who had been elected as a Member of Parliament in 1939. He scrambled after some Italian bombers in this aircraft on 19 March 1941, but when it developed engine trouble he was forced to return to Maleme. Unfortunately, a power loss on final approach caused Brabner to land short of the runway and the Buffalo overturned. Luckily, the anti-roll bar worked and the MP escaped unharmed. Brabner subsequently made his first claim over Crete and 'made ace' during the convoy battles of 1942.

10
Fulmar I N2006 of 803 NAS, flown by Lt D C E F Gibson, HMS *Formidable*, central Mediterranean, 18 April 1941
Donald Gibson had made his first claims when flying Skuas during the Norway campaign in 1940, and by early 1941 he was serving as the senior pilot of 803 NAS. He launched in this aircraft off Rhodes during the evening of 18 April 1941 at the head of a section of three Fulmars against inbound Italian bombers. Gibson led the attack on them, but N2006 was hit by return fire and he was wounded. He then headed back to his ship, and although he managed to land, the aircraft's arrestor hook pulled out and the Fulmar went over the side. Gibson was quickly rescued by a destroyer, but his observer was never seen again. The S.79 that he had attacked limped away, having also been damaged by PO Theobald – one of the Royal Navy's few NCO aces.

11
Fulmar I N1957 of 806 NAS, flown by Lt R MacDonald-Hall, HMS *Formidable*, off Crete, 26 May 1941
On the morning of 26 May 1941, Lt Bob MacDonald-Hall (in N1957) and nine-victory ace Sub Lt Graham Hogg launched off their carrier and intercepted Ju 88s inbound to the fleet. Attacking together, they set the first – probably L1+QV of LG 1 – on fire and followed it down until it crashed into the sea, its destruction making MacDonald-Hall an ace. Later in the patrol the pair attacked a second Junkers bomber and were duly credited with its destruction, although this aircraft may have also been attacked by other Fulmars. MacDonald-Hall later commanded the first Seafire squadron (807 NAS), and made the first claim with that type when he damaged a Ju 88 on 29 October 1942.

12
Sea Hurricane IB W9220 of 880 NAS, flown by Sub Lt R J Cork, Arbroath and St Merryn, March-July 1941
After its abortive re-equipment with Martlets in February

1941, 880 NAS duly received both Hurricanes and Sea Hurricanes. Amongst them was this aircraft, which was one of the first Sea Hurricanes delivered to the Royal Navy. Battle of Britain ace Dickie Cork first flew it on 7 April, and he continued to do so regularly during 880 NAS's work up training through the spring and summer. In early July it was his mount for a sustained period of air-to-air firing training, although W9220 was not among those aircraft embarked with 'A' Flight in HMS *Furious* for the Kirkenes raid that same month.

13
Martlet III AM963 of 802B Flt, flown by Sub Lt J W Sleigh, HMS *Victorious*, north Norway, September 1941
Although they had seen some action from shore bases soon after their arrival in the UK in late 1940, the Royal Navy's Martlet fighters had to wait until September 1941 to engage the enemy when flying from a carrier deck. The aircraft involved were two 802 NAS machines detached to the fleet carrier HMS *Victorious* as 802B Flt for operations off Norway. On the afternoon of 13 September, both Martlets were launched to intercept an approaching intruder, with Sub Lt Jimmy Sleigh flying this aircraft in the lead. They spotted the intruding He 111, which Sleigh successfully engaged from close range before watching the bomber plunge into the sea. On the way back to the ship he spotted another Heinkel that he attacked and damaged. Sleigh's victory was the first of many that the type would make when flying from British and American carriers in World War 2.

14
Hurricane I Z4932 of 806 NAS/RN Fighter Squadron, flown by Sub Lt M F Fell, LG123 Maddelena, Libya, 1 December 1941
In late 1941 Sub Lt Mike Fell, who was to make a total of five claims and later become an admiral, was part of the RN Fighter Squadron flying RAF Hurricanes on shipping protection duties in the western desert. On 1 December 1941, eight Hurricanes of 806 NAS engaged a formation of Ju 88s and their fighter escorts, and the Royal Navy pilots claimed a bomber and three fighters destroyed. Fell was flying this aircraft during the engagement, although he did not claim on this occasion. He first flew Z4932, which bore the name *Kiwi*, on 21 September, and then sortied in it regularly until the end of the year. The aircraft was shot down near Martuba on 15 January 1942.

15
Sea Hurricane IB AF955 of 880 NAS, flown by Lt R J Cork, HMS *Indomitable*, Diego Suarez, Madagascar, 6 May 1942
During the landings at Diego Suarez in early May 1942, the senior pilot of Sea Hurricane-equipped 880 NAS was Lt Dickie Cork. Although this was his regular aircraft, which he first flew in October 1941, Cork was in another Sea Hurricane when he led a successful strafe of the Vichy air base at Arrachart on 5 May, when he destroyed several aircraft on the ground. The following day, however, he was at the controls of AF955 when he led another strafe on a gun battery during the mopping up operations. Cork flew the aircraft for the last time on 18 June, after which the Sea Hurricane was transferred to 800 NAS.

16

Martlet II AM968 of 806 NAS, flown by Sub Lt J A Cotching, HMS *Indomitable,* Malta convoy, 12 August 1942

Although not an ace, with a total of two and two shared victories, Sub Lt John Cotching was the Royal Navy's most successful Martlet pilot. On the morning of 12 August 1942, during the crucial *Pedestal* convoy, he was flying this aircraft when he attacked a formation of S.79 torpedo-bombers and set one on fire before he ran out of ammunition – it was later confirmed as his first victory. Later that same day, Cotching again launched in AM968 and engaged the escorts for a Stuka attack. In the subsequent dogfight, he shot down Sottotenente Crimi's Re.2001. Cotching later flew Martlets during Operation *Torch* and off Norway, where he made his final claims and where he was killed in action on 8 May 1944.

17

Sea Hurricane IB Z4550 of 800 NAS, flown by Lt Cdr J M Bruen, HMS *Indomitable,* Malta convoy, 12 August 1942

'Bill' Bruen assumed command of 800 NAS aboard HMS *Indomitable* in the Indian Ocean in March 1942 – he then had four victories to his credit. In early August the ship formed part of the escort to the vital *Pedestal* convoy to the beleaguered island of Malta. Early on 12 August air attacks developed, and Bruen's 'Red' section hit a Ju 88 formation and the CO shot one of the bombers down. Two hours later, again in this aircraft, he led his section against an Italian torpedo-bomber attack, sharing in the destruction of an S.84. Bruen then went after an S.79 flying at low level, his fire causing it to plunge into the sea. 'Bill' Bruen's victories during the day thus made him an ace.

18

Martlet IV FN112 of 888 NAS, flown by Lt D M Jeram, HMS *Formidable,* Operation *Torch,* 6 November 1943

Lt Denis Jeram is believed to have been flying this Martlet on a combat air patrol from *Formidable* on 6 November 1942 – just prior to the Allied landings in North Africa – when he was ordered to intercept Vichy-French aircraft. He caught what he thought was a Potez Po.63 (it was actually a Bloch MB.174 of GR II/52) on a reconnaissance flight off Cape Khamis, in Algeria, at 10,000 ft, and in a brief engagement sent it down to claim his fifth victory. Like other Royal Navy aircraft involved in *Torch*, FN112 had had its roundels over-painted with US stars. On 9 November Jeram used another Martlet to share in the destruction of a Ju 88 – his final claim. A few minutes earlier, FN112, flown by Sub Lt P D Street, had shared in the destruction of a He 111.

19

Sea Hurricane IIB JS355 of 800 NAS, flown by Lt Cdr J M Bruen, HMS *Biter,* Operation *Torch,* 8 November 1943

Lt Cdr 'Bill' Bruen's 800 NAS also had the roundels on its Sea Hurricanes overpainted with US stars on the eve of *Torch* so as to give the impression of an American-only operation. Bruen launched before dawn, leading part of the escort for Albacores sent to dive-bomb La Senia airfield, in Oran. Approaching the target, the Royal Navy biplanes were attacked by Vichy D.520 fighters, and Bruen led his Sea Hurricanes to the rescue. Seeing a Dewoitine on the tail of an Albacore, he came in high from astern the French fighter and

put an accurate stream of fire into the D.520's engine which burst into flames. The pilot immediately baled out, giving 'Bill' Bruen his eighth, and last, victory.

20

Corsair II JT269 of the 15th Naval Fighter Wing, flown by Lt Cdr R J Cork, HMS *Illustrious,* Indian Ocean, March-April 1944

The Wing Leader of the Corsair-equipped 15th Naval Fighter Wing aboard HMS *Illustrious* was one of the Royal Navy's great fighter leaders, and earliest aces, Lt Cdr Dickie Cork. The wing comprised 1830 and 1833 NASs, and the ship formed part of the Eastern Fleet that was building in Ceylon. Cork was allocated JT269 as his personal aircraft, which he adorned with his initials – a rare feature on Royal Navy aircraft. In keeping with RAF practice in-theatre, the red of the roundels was also deleted. Cork took over this aircraft when it was first delivered, and only flew others when it was being serviced. He was, however, flying JT347 when, on 14 April 1944, he was killed in a landing accident at China Bay.

21

Hellcat I JV132 of 800 NAS, flown by Lt B Ritchie, HMS *Emperor,* central Norway, 8 May 1944

Blythe Ritchie gained four victories whilst flying Sea Hurricanes with 800 NAS in 1942, and he was still serving with the unit in mid-1944. The squadron had by then re-equipped with the superb Hellcat, but the type had little opportunity to test its mettle against Luftwaffe fighters. One of the few times that the Grumman fighter encountered German aircraft came on 8 May 1944, when Ritchie was flying this aircraft on a sweep off Norway. His unit was attacked by Bf 109s and Fw 190s from JG 5, and in the brief combat which ensued, one of the Fw 190s fell to Ritchie's guns, which took him to acedom. Six days later he was again in JV132 when *Emperor's* Hellcats attacked a formation of He 115 floatplanes, and the Scot shot one down and shared in the destruction of another with fellow ace Lt Cdr Stan Orr. These were Ritchie's final victories.

22

Hellcat I JV125 of 804 NAS, flown by Lt Cdr S G Orr, HMS *Emperor,* central Norway, 14 May 1944

As mentioned in the notes for the previous profile, on 14 May 1944, Hellcats from *Emperor's* 800 and 804 NASs, led by the CO of the latter unit, Lt Cdr Stan Orr (in this aircraft), were on an anti-shipping strike when they spotted a formation of five He 115 floatplanes low over the sea off Rorvik. Orr and future ace Lt Ritchie of 800 NAS combined to shoot one down, Ritchie having already despatched another Heinkel. The surviving floatplanes quickly alighted on the sea, and Orr then led the Hellcats down to destroy them on the water – he duly shared in the destruction of two more. These were Orr's final air combat success, taking his tally to 12 destroyed, of which six were shared. These were also the last victories that Royal Navy Hellcats claimed against the Luftwaffe.

23

Mosquito XVII HK252 of No 125 Sqn, flown by Sub Lt M H J Petrie, Hurn, 22 June 1944

In 1943-44, a number of Royal Navy fighter crews were

seconded to RAF Mosquito nightfighter squadrons to gain experience in the role prior to the Fleet Air Arm conducting nocturnal missions from its carriers. Several of these crews gained a number of successes during this time, including New Zealander Sub Lt Malcolm Petrie and his observer Lt F A Noyes. They served with No 125 (Newfoundland) Sqn, based on the south coast for defence of the huge D-Day fleet prior to the invasion of France. Allocated HK252, the pair flew this Mosquito for the first time on 29 March 1944 and performed a defensive patrol with it over the Channel on 5 June. Seventeen days later, off the coast of Fecamp, north of Le Havre, Petrie and Noyes downed two Ju 88s attempting to attack offshore shipping. These were Petrie's only claims.

24
Corsair II JT361 of 1834 NAS, flown by Lt Cdr P N Charlton, HMS *Victorious*, Indian Ocean, August-September 1944

During operations over Norway, the Mediterranean and the desert, Noel Charlton had gained six victories, and in December 1943 he was given command of Corsair-equipped 1834 NAS. Subsequently leading the unit in the *Tirpitz* strikes, Charlton and 1834 NAS then sailed with *Victorious* into the Indian Ocean and participated in the Sabang raid. To coincide with the American landings at Peleliu in September 1944, *Victorious* and *Indomitable* sallied for another diversionary attack on Sumatra. On the 18th, at the controls of JT361, Charlton led his squadron on a strike on the railway repair yard at Sigli. Upon his return to the carrier, Charlton discovered that his drop tank would not release, and when the aircraft caught the arrestor wire on deck it broke away and burst into flames – fortunately he was uninjured. The aircraft was duly repaired, but was eventually written off on 1 January 1945 in a heavy landing by Lt Peter Carmichael, who would later shoot down a MiG-15 over Korea whilst flying a Sea Fury.

25
Corsair II JT427 of the 47th Naval Fighter Wing, flown by Maj R C Hay, HMS *Victorious*, Andaman and Nicobar Islands, 17-19 October 1944

Ronnie Hay began flying operations on Skuas in 1940, and by the summer of 1945 was serving as the air coordinator and leader of the 47th NFW. Allocated JT427 in September as his personal aircraft, Hay adorned it with his initials in place of the unit codes. He flew it during the strikes on Car Nicobar in October, and also when he acted as the air coordinator for the devastating attacks on the Japanese-held oil refineries in Sumatra in January 1945. During one of the latter missions, on the 24th, he destroyed a Ki-43 and a Ki-44 over Tandjoengradja. Five days later, Hay shared in the destruction of another 'Oscar' and 'Tojo' to take his score to 13. Although he saw further service during Okinawa operations, he made no additional claims. The only Royal Marine ace, Hay was one of the few Allied pilots to have downed aircraft from all the main protagonists – Germany, Italy, Vichy France and Japan.

26
Corsair II JT383 of 1834 NAS, flown by Sub Lt L D Durno, HMS *Victorious*, Andaman and Nicobar Islands, 19 October 1944

Canadian Leslie Durno is one of the Royal Navy's least known

aces who participated in Operation *Millet*, which was a diversionary strike on Car Nicobar in mid October 1944. At around 0840 hrs on the 19th, the fleet was located by the Japanese and one hour later it was attacked by a dozen Ki-43s of the 1st Reserve Flying Unit. In a fierce 40-minute fight, the enemy was driven off, but at the cost of two Corsairs and a Hellcat. However, flying this aircraft in his first action, Leslie Durno shot down one of the Ki-43s and shared in the destruction of two more with Sub Lt Grave. He may have also flown JT383 on the first of the Sumatran oil strikes on 4 January 1945, when he shared in the destruction of a Ki-21 and a Ki-46 – these kills gave him ace status.

27
Hellcat II FN439 of 1844 NAS, flown by Lt K A McLennan, HMS *Indomitable*, Sumatra, January 1945

New Zealander Keith McLennan joined Hellcat-equipped 1844 NAS after completing his flying training, and duly took part in operations in the Indian Ocean in 1944. He made his first claim during the Royal Navy's opening strike on Palembang on 4 January 1945. On the final strike, on the 29th, McLennan was on deck alert in FN439/R5K when seven Ki-21 'Sally' and Ki-48 'Lily' bombers of the 'Shichisi Mitate' Special Attack Corps attempted to make low-level suicide attacks on the fleet. Hastily launched, he destroyed two Ki-21s and shared a third with a Seafire, as all seven bombers were downed. McLennan was Mentioned in Despatches, and these victories took his total to 3$\frac{1}{2}$ destroyed, thus making him the most successful Royal New Zealand Navy pilot of World War 2.

28
Corsair II JT410 of 1836 NAS, flown by Sub Lt D J Sheppard, HMS *Victorious*, Sumatra, January 1945

Canadian Don Sheppard began flying Corsairs after training, eventually joining 1836 NAS, with whom he took part in the *Tirpitz* attacks. On the first strike on the Sumatran oil refineries, he was flying this aircraft as part of the close escort, and he managed to shoot down two Ki-43s. During the next attack on Palembang, on the 24th, Sheppard was again flying JT410 as part of the escort when he attacked and hit a Ki-44, which was initially credited as a probable but is thought to have later been confirmed. Sheppard again flew this Corsair during the last strike on the oil refineries five days later when, near the target, he reached acedom by sharing in the destruction of two more Ki-44s with Maj Ronnie Hay. JT410 had also been used by another pilot to shoot down a Ki-43 over Car Nicobar the previous October.

29
Seafire III PR256 of 894 NAS, flown by Sub Lt R H Reynolds, HMS *Indefatigable*, Okinawa, 1 April 1945

When he sailed with the Fleet to support the US landings on Okinawa, Richard Reynolds already had two shared victories to his credit. Because of their limited range, the Seafires were used for fleet defence only, and early on 1 April 1945, an inbound *kamikaze* raid was intercepted by the Seafire CAP. One Zero dived towards *Indefatigable*, with Reynolds on its tail, and in spite of its evasion, and proximity to the barrage, the Seafire pilot continued attacking. Indeed, he only broke away just prior to the Japanese fighter hitting the ship. Reynolds was given a half share in the Zero. Twenty minutes later he attacked a second Zero, and with two short bursts sent it down. He then chased another, using up his remaining ammunition to send his third victim down. In so doing Reynolds became the Royal Navy's only Seafire ace. PR256 was quickly decorated with its pilot's score, as shown here, and the fighter survived the war.

30
Hellcat II JX886 of 1839 NAS, flown by Sub Lt E T Wilson, HMS *Indomitable*, Okinawa, 6 April 1945
Although on strength with 1839 NAS on 6 April 1945, JX886 was flown by six-victory ace Sub Lt Edward Wilson of 1844 NAS on this date. Tasked with attacking airfields on the Sakishima Gunto archipelago to prevent Japanese air movement from Formosa to Okinawa, Wilson was leading a section which included future ace Sub Lt Bill Atkinson. About 100 miles south of Nansei Shoto, they downed a D4Y 'Judy' to give Wilson his final victory. He was one of a number of South African Naval Force pilots to fly with the Royal Navy, although only he 'made ace'. Six days later, JX886 was used by another pilot to down a Ki-43 off Formosa.

31
Firefly I DV119 of 1770 NAS, flown by Sub Lt J P Stott, HMS *Indefatigable*, Okinawa, 12 April 1945
As the excellent Firefly was mainly used as a strike aircraft, its opportunities for air combat were limited. Nevertheless, their BPF pilots did make a number of claims. For example, during operations off Formosa on 12 April 1945, a pair of Fireflies (one of them being DV119, flown by Sub Lt Phil Stott and his observer Lt B Ward) were escorting a US Navy Mariner flying-boat on an air-sea rescue mission when they spotted five Ki-51 'Sonia' light bombers. The fighters immediately broke away and attacked, and each of the Firefly pilots shot down two bombers apiece. Stott, who had claimed three shared victories during the attacks on Sumatra the previous January, thus became the Navy's first, and only, Firefly ace.

32
Hellcat II JX814 of 1844 NAS, flown by Sub Lt W M C Foster, HMS *Indomitable*, Okinawa, 12 April 1945
Having shared in the destruction of an 'Oscar' during the attacks on Palembang in January 1945, Bill Foster had further opportunities to add to his tally during the BPF's operations over the Sakishima Gunto in April. Soon after dawn on 12 April, when flying this aircraft during operations off Formosa, Foster was launched from *Indomitable* against Japanese aircraft. He initially encountered a Ki-61, which he shot down, and then followed this up shortly afterwards with a Ki-43. Before the end of the Okinawa operation, Foster had made two further claims to become one of the Royal Navy's few Hellcat aces. His aircraft was not so fortunate, however, as it flew into the fleet flak barrage on 13 April whilst being flown by Canadian pilot Lt Thurston. The latter was chasing a Japanese aircraft at the time.

33
Corsair II JT537 of 1836 NAS, flown by Sub Lt D J Sheppard, HMS *Victorious*, Okinawa, 4 May 1945
Having become an ace over Sumatra, Sub Lt Don Sheppard was still with the British Pacific Fleet when it began operations supporting the invasion of Okinawa. Although the fighter squadrons mainly flew ground attack missions, they also claimed a significant number of successes during *kamikaze* attacks on the fleet. Sheppard used JT537 to destroy a D4Y 'Judy' torpedo-bomber during one such attack on 4 May, the fire from his six 0.50-in guns causing it to break up and crash into the sea for his final victory. By this stage Royal Navy aircraft wore US-style barred markings and carried identity numbers and ship fin codes, rather than unit codes.

34
Seafire III NN621 of 880 NAS, flown by Lt Cdr R M Crosley, HMS *Implacable*, Japan, August 1945
Having become an ace over Normandy, Mike Crosley was given command of 880 NAS shortly afterwards. He then embarked with the unit in HMS *Implacable*, which in turn joined the BPF following the Okinawa operation. Once in the Pacific, *Implacable*'s Seafires were fitted with disused P-40 drop tanks to extend their range, and NN621 became Crosley's regular aircraft. Although he flew it on a number of 'Ramrods' over the Japanese home islands during July and August 1945, Crosley used PR259 to make his final claims when he destroyed a 'Pete' floatplane and damaged a 'Mavis' flying-boat on the ground in late July. As well as standard BPF markings, NN621 was decorated with a blue spinner and a blue rudder with a vertical white stripe.

35
Corsair IV KD658 of 1841 NAS, flown by Lt R H Gray, HMS *Formidable*, Japan, 9 August 1945
The Corsair was to play a key role in the attacks launched by the BPF against the Japanese home islands in July and August 1945. One of the units involved in these strikes was 1841 NAS, whose senior pilot was Canadian Lt 'Hammy' Gray. Airfields and shipping proved to be favourite targets for the marauding Corsair pilots, and on 28 July Gray led a low-level strike against the naval base at Maisuru, north of Kyoto – he was awarded a DSC for is efforts during this mission. Gray's usual aircraft at this time was KD560, but on 9 August, when he led yet another 'Ramrod', he was at the controls of this aircraft, KD658. Whilst overflying Onagawa Wan Bay, Gray spotted two destroyers and escorts, and he led the attack in the face of a very heavy fire and sank the escort *Amasuka*. He was shot down in the process, however, and for his gallantry, Gray was posthumously awarded the VC.

36
Seafire III NN300 of 807 NAS/4th NFW, flown by Lt Cdr G C Baldwin, HMS *Hunter*, Singapore, September 1945
Seafires of the 4th NFW, under its leader Lt Cdr George Baldwin, conducted operations along the Burmese coast, harrying the retreating Japanese. During a rare contact with enemy aircraft, on 16 May two Seafires from 807 NAS (including NN300) damaged a pair of Ki-43s. Although on the strength of his old unit, NN300 became Baldwin's personal mount, and as such it was stripped of its camouflage and had black identity markings and codes applied. It was used by him when the carrier returned to Singapore to re-occupy the island. Baldwin had flown Skuas and Rocs over Norway in 1940 and claimed the Seafire's first confirmed victory in 1942.

Bibliography

Banks, Capt R D, *From Whitecaps to Contrails.* CFB Shearwater, 1981

Brown, David, *Carrier Operations of World War 2 Vol 1.* Ian Allan, 1968 & 1974

Brown, David, *The British Pacific & East Indies Fleets.* Brodie, 1995

Brown, David, *The Seafire.* Ian Allan, 1973

Cameron, Ian, *Wings of the Morning.* Hodder & Stoughton, 1962

Crosley, Cdr R M, *They Gave Me a Seafire.* Airlife, 1986 & 2001

Flintham, Vic & Thomas, Andrew, *Combat Codes.* Airlife, 2003

Gibson, Vice Admiral Sir Donald, *Hold Taut & Belay!* Spellmount, 1992

Jameson, Rear Admiral William, *Ark Royal.* Hart-Davis, 1957

MOI, *The Fleet Air Arm.* HMSO, 1943

Moore, John, *The Fleet Air Arm.* Chapman & Hall, 1943

Shores, Christopher, *Fighters over Tunisia.* Neville Spearman, 1974

Shores, Christopher, *Those Other Eagles.* Grub Street, 2004

Shores, Christopher, Cull, Brian with Malizia, Nicola, *Malta – The Hurricane Years.* Grub Street, 1987

Shores, Christopher, Cull, Brian with Malizia, Nicola, *Air War for Yugoslavia, Greece & Crete.* Grub Street, 1987

Shores, Christopher, Cull, Brian with Malizia, Nicola, *Malta – The Spitfire Year.* Grub Street, 1991

Shores, Christopher et al, *Fledgling Eagles.* Grub Street, 1991

Shores, Christopher et al, *Dust Clouds in the Middle East.* Grub Street, 1996 & 1999

Shores, Christopher et al, *Bloody Shambles Vol 2.* Grub Street, 1993

Shores, Christopher & Williams, Clive, *Aces High Vols 1 & 2.* Grub Street, 1994

Soward, Stuart E, *A Formidable Hero.* CANAV Books, 1987

Sturtivant, Ray, *Fleet Air Arm at War.* Ian Allan, 1982

Sturtivant, Ray & Balance, Theo, *The Squadrons of the Fleet Air Arm.* Air Britain, 1994

Sturtivant, Ray & Burrow, Mick, *Fleet Air Arm Aircraft 1939-1945.* Air Britain, 1995

Styling, Mark, *Aircraft of the Aces 8 – Corsair Aces of World War 2.* Osprey, 1995

Tillman, Barrett, *Aircraft of the Aces 3 – Wildcat Aces of World War 2.* Osprey, 1995

Tillman, Barrett, *Aircraft of the Aces 10 – Hellcat Aces of World War 2.* Osprey, 1996

Winton, John, *Find, Fix & Strike!* Batsford, 1980

INDEX

References to illustrations are shown in **bold**. Plates are shown with page and caption locators in (brackets).